50 Things to Think About as an Early Career Researcher

Paving Your Way to Success

Margaret J. Robertson,
Donna Starks, and Gaelle Horsley

LONDON AND NEW YORK

Designed cover image: Getty Images

First published 2026
by Routledge
4 Park Square, Milton Park, Abingdon, Oxon OX14 4RN

and by Routledge
605 Third Avenue, New York, NY 10158

Routledge is an imprint of the Taylor & Francis Group, an informa business

© 2026 Margaret J. Robertson, Donna Starks, and Gaelle Horsley

The right of Margaret J. Robertson, Donna Starks, and Gaelle Horsley to be identified as authors of this work has been asserted in accordance with sections 77 and 78 of the Copyright, Designs and Patents Act 1988.

All rights reserved. No part of this book may be reprinted or reproduced or utilised in any form or by any electronic, mechanical, or other means, now known or hereafter invented, including photocopying and recording, or in any information storage or retrieval system, without permission in writing from the publishers.

Trademark notice: Product or corporate names may be trademarks or registered trademarks, and are used only for identification and explanation without intent to infringe.

British Library Cataloguing-in-Publication Data
A catalogue record for this book is available from the British Library

ISBN: 978-1-032-77054-3 (hbk)
ISBN: 978-1-032-77053-6 (pbk)
ISBN: 978-1-003-48103-4 (ebk)

DOI: 10.4324/9781003481034

Typeset in Optima
by codeMantra

"*50 Things to Think About as an Early Career Researcher* is a game changer. During my Ph.D. final year and my early career transition, navigating the unwritten rules and hidden wisdom of practice and being an early academic researcher felt overwhelming. This book changes that dynamic! The authors have skilfully distilled scattered insights into one accessible guide, making the journey not just 'survivable' but 'actionable'. Whether you are starting out or supporting emerging researchers, this book is an essential companion – one that belongs on your desk."

Nick Baker, *Lecturer, Otago University, New Zealand*

"Completing your PhD and becoming an ECR can pose huge challenges to your identity – who are you now? *50 Things to Think About as an Early Career Researcher: Paving Your Way to Success* is packed full of practical suggestions about how to successfully navigate this change and build your research career. Presented in an approachable, easy-to-read style, the authors offer timeless advice in response to a fast-changing research environment. The clear structure lays out common issues facing today's ECRs, offering ideas about how to leverage doctoral experience and progress your research in new and satisfying directions."

Cally Guerin, *Senior Lecturer, Graduate Research School, La Trobe University, Australia*

"This book reflects the wisdom and experience of academics who have clearly guided and mentored many over the years. Written with deep empathy, it acknowledges the unique challenges and diverse paths each early career researcher may take, making it relatable for anyone navigating this phase. As an early career researcher myself, I found the advice not only resonates with my current experiences but also offers guidance for what lies ahead. It's a resource I'll continue to return to as I grow in my professional journey."

Jessica Velasquez Urribarri, *Lecturer, University of Adelaide, Australia*

50 Things to Think About as an Early Career Researcher

This book for Early Career Researchers (ECRs) provides vital insights for jump-starting your research career and guidance on how you can find your own ways of knowing, being, doing, and communicating to progress your career.

Charting a course through the first years of a research career, while retaining control of your life and your authenticity is more challenging than it has ever been. This book argues that there are multiple ways of being an ECR, and that research pathways are uniquely individual. It shows how to prepare yourself for your research journey and contains useful hints about preparing manuscripts, writing research grants, developing supervision skills, and forging a successful research career. Offering solutions to common challenges, it provides insights into preparing CVs, preparing for interviews and other opportunities for you and your career.

Providing practical advice based on extensive experience, this book is essential reading for those completing, or who have recently completed, PhDs, as well as those in the early stages of their career in higher education.

Margaret J. Robertson is an Honorary Academic at La Trobe University School of Education. Her research focus is team supervision and agency development within this context. Her recent research considers the importance of agency through education, life and career choices, and the importance of role models.

Donna Starks is an Honorary Researcher in the School of Cultures, Languages and Linguistics at The University of Auckland. Her research focuses on how we manifest ourselves through our ways of knowing, being, and communicating to the world around us.

Gaelle Horsley is a Master of Social Work, though originally qualified to teach art and English, in the UK. She has recently retired from sessional tutoring in Counselling at Victoria University, and now teaches beginner and advanced watercolours at Hunt Club Arts Centre (Brimbank Council).

Contents

List of Figures	x
Acknowledgment to country	xi
Acknowledgments	xii

1. Introduction — 1
  Overview — 1
  Why this book? — 1
  Guidebooks for early career research — 2
  How to read this book — 4
  What each chapter in our book offers — 6

2. Preparing for the ECR journey ahead — 9
  Overview — 9
  Transitioning from thesis writer to ECR — 10
  Your ways of knowing — 11
  Your ways of being and doing — 12
  Your ways of communicating — 13

3. Building your research career — 16
  Overview — 16
  1. No two ECRs are alike — 17
  2. What's your brand? — 19
  3. What's your social media strategy? — 21
  4. Using conferences to promote your brand — 24
  5. What do you imagine 'success' to be? — 27
  6. Taking care of yourself in research — 29
  Notes — 31

Contents

4. Collaborations — 32
Overview — 32
7. Co-authoring — 33
8. Mentors — 35
9. Developing support networks — 37
10. Using administrative committee work to further your career — 40
11. Finding yourself within institutional brands — 42
Notes — 43

5. Your research: Publication — 44
Overview — 44
12. What's your publication plan? — 45
13. Making an impact through your publications — 47
14. Choosing publication formats for your publication plan — 49
15. Choose your journal then write your manuscript — 56
16. Hints for writing: getting published — 58
17. Receiving feedback — 60
18. Your voice in publications — 62
19. Turning reviewer comments into new writing ideas — 64
Note — 66

6. Progressing your research with (or without) funding — 67
Overview — 67
20. Working as part of someone else's team — 68
21. Starting on your own with unfunded research — 69
22. Working with community-based research — 72
23. Exploring all possible funding — 74
24. Assessing grants for the right fit — 76
25. Crowdfunding your research project — 78
26. Writing your funding proposal so that it sells — 80
27. Writing yourself and your team into your funding applications — 83
28. Preparing your budget — 85
29. Taking your project through to completion — 88
Notes — 92

7. You as a supervisor — 93
Overview — 93
30. Understanding you as a supervisor — 94
31. Choosing research candidates that build your research profile — 96
32. Setting up successful supervision sessions — 98

33. Successfully co-supervising	100
34. Co-publishing with supervisees	102
Notes	105

8. Difficulties — 106

Overview	106
35. Your co-author(s) are driving you nuts!	107
36. Your manuscripts take too much time to write	110
37. The review process is taking forever	112
38. Conflicting reviewer comments	114
39. Your revisions exceed mandated word (or page) limits	117
40. Your grant application was not accepted	119
41. Your grant got reduced funding	121
42. Your principal supervisor is causing you headaches	123
43. Supervising doctoral 'orphans'	126

9. Next steps — 129

Overview	129
44. Writing yourself into your CV	130
45. Using sessional work to your advantage	132
46. Is a post-doc for you?	134
47. Building resilience: missing out and nailing it next time	136
48. Promotion	139
49. Changing career direction	142
50. Taking care of yourself	145

Afterword: using Artificial Intelligence (AI) in research	149
References	153
Index	163

Figures

2.1	The new 'you'	9
3.1	No two ECRs are alike	16
4.1	Collaborating will help you progress	32
5.1	What's your publication plan?	44
6.1	Small successes lead to bigger grants	67
7.1	How well can you align your research plan and potential research candidates?	93
8.1	Things don't always go to plan!	106
9.1	What steps do you want to take?	129
9.2	What sign do you have on your door?	146

# Acknowledgment to country

We acknowledge the traditional custodians of the lands on which this book was written – the Wurundjeri Woi-wurrung and Bunurong Boon Wurrung peoples of Naam Melbourne, and the Yugambeh peoples of the Bundjalung nation of Coolangatta.

We pay respects to their elders past and present and acknowledge that land was never ceded.

Acknowledgments

Thanks go to our families for their persistence in imposing balance in our lives while we wrote this volume. The distractions of minding pets, moving or renovating the house, flying overseas for family visits, and regular workouts on the farm kept us fresh and eager to return to the computer and write.

We are also grateful to friends and colleagues who were remarkably willing to inquire about progress and shared the angst of multiple rewrites and reconfigurations as this book took shape. A special thank you to friends, family, and colleagues who have made suggestions for improvements to our work.

We would also like to thank the Routledge Editorial team in Melbourne: Vilija Stephens and Georgia Oman for working with us when our writing plans went seriously off the rails with health issues. We appreciated your support, professionalism, and patience while we got back on task.

# Introduction

Overview

This chapter presents an overview of existing literature in Early Career Research (ECR) and clarifies the book's focus. It explains why you as an ECR need to take your own pathway for your career success and wellbeing. No two ECRs are alike.

Why this book?

This is our second book. In our first book, *50 Things to Think About When Writing a Thesis,* we explored how each thesis writer was unique with their own ways of researching, writing, and being supervised. That book focused on how thesis writers should feel able to write themselves into their work and control their own thesis journey. After we published our book, we received comments about how a similar book would be useful for ECRs. This book is our response to these requests. It explores the challenge of becoming an ECR.

As an ECR you will experience change. New relationships with your thesis supervisors will need to be developed. You will need to find and potentially develop additional forms of mentoring and support. You will face challenges as you fill gaps in your ways of knowing and doing. These gaps might involve grant writing or being a part of (or leading) a research team. They may be in your writing experience. You may have limited experience in co-authoring, or you may have yet to publish at all. Manuscripts differ from theses and come with different expectations that take time to master.

As an ECR, you are often expected to supervise, requiring an identity shift from supervisee to supervisor. As an ECR, you may have personal wants and needs (i.e., family, health issues, travel) that may have changed since your days as a doctoral candidate.

This book aims to help you cope with change and fill in gaps in your ways of knowing, doing, and communicating to help you on your journey to a successful career.

Guidebooks for early career research

You will find many guidebooks on the market. No book has all the answers. For this reason, it is useful to look at various works that give advice to researchers, consider what they have to offer, and where our book fits in among them.

Some guidebooks offer advice designed for all researchers. Williams, Jones, and Robertson (2014) is one such example. Their advice is not directed toward any stage of an academic career. Guidebooks don't have to list 'Early Career Researcher' in the title to be useful, but it is sometimes nice to pick up a book where you know the advice therein is meant for you.

Some guidebooks are designed for ECRs, but they are not all the same. Some consider ECRs to include both thesis writers and those who recently completed their doctoral thesis (i.e., McAlpine & Åkerlind, 2010). This approach is a useful starting point as both thesis writers and those who have completed doctorates are at the beginning of their research careers and often share trepidation about that research journey and how to navigate it. Both thesis writers and those who have completed doctorates are new to the publication game. Both have limited experience applying for grants. Both experience similar setbacks (i.e., rejected manuscripts and manuscript revisions). Both can encounter emotional difficulties with being in a world of research that their family and significant others may not fully understand. While the advice in these guidebooks tends to cover issues that both thesis writers and ECRs want to know about, these guidebooks also typically contain chapters devoted to issues that pertain only to thesis writers, such as supervision (i.e., Roche, 2022) and tips about thesis writing (i.e., Eley et al., 2012). If you are an ECR who has completed a thesis, only some parts of these books will be relevant to you.

Other guidebooks are designed for those ECRs who have completed their doctorates. This is the ECR we consider in this book. While thesis writers and those who have completed a thesis share similarities, there are important differences. Your successful completion of a doctorate means you have become part of a different research community. You have a new identity and can embark on different research activities. You can apply for a wider range of permanent academic positions, post-docs, author and co-author on a wider range of topics, and even serve as lead researchers in grant applications. Having completed your thesis, you have demonstrated that you can safely conduct research and create new knowledge. You are a new you.

Guidebooks come in two forms: authored works and edited volumes. There are a wealth of each. To name a few, authored works include Bataille and Brown (2006), Cantwell and Scevak (2010), Clews (2021), Debowski (2012), Johnson (2011), McAlpine and Amundsen (2018), and Roberts and Wilty (2017). Edited works include Denholm and Evans (2009), Kwasnicka and Lai (2022), Mahat and Tatebe (2019), Murgia and Poggio (2019), Singh (2022), and Thwaites and Pressland (2017). The authored volumes often cover a range of issues, while the edited volumes tend to give personal accounts of specific issues encountered by individual researchers. The latter can be comforting to read if you feel isolated and alone when facing ECR challenges.

Guidebooks also differ in their content. Some guidebooks such as those listed earlier provide a broad range of academic advice. Our book falls into this category. Other guidebooks provide in-depth advice on specific topics in the ECR journey. Some guidebooks concentrate on general academic concerns, such as methodological issues in social research (Ajebon, Kwong, & Astorga de Ita, 2021). Others have a wider focus. Zimmerman (2021) provides insights into methodology approaches, research, and writing. Those who consider academic concerns focus on specific issues such as digital research spaces (Costa & Condie, 2018), grant writing (Khoo, Ward & O'Donnell, 2023), and the publication game (Clews, 2021; Dunleavy & Tinkler, 2021; Habibie & Burgess, 2021; Neave, Connor & Crawford, 2007). Paltridge (2017) addresses the role of peer review in journal publications, Burford and Henderson (2023) advise on presenting, participating, and organizing academic conferences, Pommerening (2021) explores mentoring, while Lemon and Salmons (2021) delve into issues surrounding working collaboratively. Boynton (2020) concentrates on staying well through it all.

Other specialized guidebooks cover employment issues to help you in your quest for that dream job. Denicolo and Reeves (2013), for example, consider ways of improving your future employment opportunities within and outside the university. Denholm and Evans (2009) examine leveraging your thesis to open up a wide range of employment opportunities. Roche (2022) delves into online resources that support skills development. Some explore alternative employment contexts. Jaeger and Dinin (2018) consider post-doc work. Spina et al. (2020), contract work and Singh (2022), the increasing need for global mobility.

Finally, some specialized guidebooks concentrate on ECR identity issues. For example, Murgia and Poggio (2019) explore the trajectory of women in the academy and Thwaites and Pressland (2017) examine the intense pressures and demands on female early career academics. Guidebooks on identity tend to explore the needs of ECR through personal stories. Kwasnicka and Lai (2022) take this approach to frame advice for ECRs about working in academic and other research environments. McAlpine and Amundsen (2018) likewise embrace diversity as they probe into, and document, the identity trajectories of 48 ECRs over ten years. The latter work highlights career decision-making and is a good illustration of how ECR identities can change over time. McAlpine and Amundsen's work takes as its fundamental concern that identities are fluid, multiple, and no single set of advice can fit all. This is the position we take in our book.

How to read this book

This book's content is designed to be read in three different ways. If you are embarking on your ECR journey and unsure how to proceed, you could read our book from beginning to end, as you would other books cited in our literature review. Reading in this way can give ideas about how to design your ECR journey at the outset of your ECR career. If you need a quick fix and are unsure about an aspect of your career, you can read a particular chapter.

Like many other books, you can also pick up our book and read a chapter when you have a particular concern. The book covers a range of issues for career success.

However, unlike most guidebooks, there is a third dimension to this book. It is designed around pointers to suit ECRs with different levels of confidence, training, ability, experience, time, and different needs. For example, maybe you already feel at home in your ongoing position and have a well-developed research agenda ahead of you but want a few quick ideas about how to bring things together or give you that edge in what you are looking for. Maybe you are working entirely outside academia and need advice on how to begin a research career, and secure research funds. Or perhaps you have a teaching only position and want to know how to embed research into your teaching. Perhaps your needs are personal. You may be a parent or responsible for caring for relatives and need a few ideas about how you can best work in this situation. You may be in a contract position that you hope will lead to a tenured position and you want advice to take into your job interview. Or maybe you have been employed in a series of short term research positions and need to make connections between the different types of research that you have been doing. Because we recognize that ECRs are often time poor, we have attempted to compose the book as an easy read. Each pointer is short, packed with suggestions, and with recommended reading if you are keen to get more information on a given topic.

Because the ECR journey is a transformative process, you can return to the book to read the same or different pointers at various points in your career. You can see yourself in a very different light and feel the need to grab onto very different pieces of information as you move forward. At times in your research journey, you may see your research as your primary driving force in life, at other times you might just want to keep your research bubbling along, perhaps publishing work out of your thesis, while you find a suitable job or take care of yourself or your family. The book is designed to offer suggestions to cater to different needs at different times in your career.

Whatever your situation, the book aspires to help you grow in confidence as a researcher and writer, develop resilience, conquer your fears, and deal with challenges when they arise by making small changes to how you think about who you are as a researcher and who you want to be. As we pointed out in our previous volume *50 Things to Think About When Writing a Thesis*, small changes to how you work have the potential to make big differences to how you feel about your identity, and this, in turn, affects how you project who you are to your colleagues, reviewers, and even your supervisees. Acknowledging your individual ways of knowing, being, doing, and communicating, and maintaining a pathway toward success can be difficult. Our goal is to help you on that journey.

What each chapter in our book offers

The first chapter explains what the book is about so you can decide if the book is useful for you. Chapter 2 asks you as an ECR to consider how your past thesis writing identities differ from your imagined, emerging, and existing identities as an ECR and the changes you might want to make. It explores how your existing and imagined ways of knowing, being, doing, and communicating can be used to empower you on your ECR journey. The remainder of the book consists of 50 pointers, each designed as a quick fix to kickstart your career in ways that fit with your identity and your ways of knowing, being, doing, and communicating. The first set of pointers, covered in Chapters 3 and 4, focus on you, your career planning, and getting support to help you along the way. The pointers in Chapters 5, 6, and 7 turn to consider three central issues in the ECR journey: publications, funding, and supervision, and explore how you can focus your journey on ways of being and doing that work for you. Chapter 8 shifts to take a different approach. It offers suggestions for dealing with situations that do not go as planned and when parts of your career veer off track to pick yourself up and move forward. Chapter 9 ends the volume with pointers on career progression. The pointers include practical advice on CV preparation, career direction, and thoughts on getting a promotion. This chapter ends with its most important point, the need to take care of yourself. To forge a successful career, you need to be healthy in body and mind. The risks are great if you compromise either.

References

Ajebon, Mildred Oiza; Kwong, Yim Ming Connie, & Astorga de Ita, Diego. (2021). *Navigating the field: Postgraduate experiences in social research*. Springer Nature. https://doi.org/10.1007/978-3-030-68113-5

Bataille, Gretchen M., & Brown, Betsy E. (2006). *Faculty career paths: Multiple routes to academic success and satisfaction*. Rowman and Littlefield.

Boynton, Petra. (2020). *Being well in academia: Ways to feel stronger, safer and more connected*. Routledge. https://doi.org/10.4324/9780429197512

Burford, James, & Henderson, Emily F. (2023). *Making sense of academic conferences: Presenting, participating and organising*. Routledge. https://doi.org/10.4324/9781003144885

Cantwell, Robert Harley, & Scevak, Jill Janina (Eds.). (2010). *An academic life: A handbook for new academics*. Aust Council for Ed Research.

Clews, Simon. (2021). *The new academic: How to write, present and profile your amazing research to the world*. NewSouth Publishing.

Costa, Cristina, & Condie, Jenna. (2018). *Doing research in and on the digital: Research methods across fields of enquiry*. Routledge. https://doi.org/10.4324/9781315561622

Debowski, Shelda. (2012). *The new academic: A strategic handbook*. Open University Press.

Denholm, Carey, & Evans, Terry (Eds.). (2009). *Beyond doctorates downunder: Maximising the impact of your doctorate from Australia and New Zealand*. (2nd ed.) ACER.

Denicolo, Pam, & Reeves, Julie. (2013). *Developing transferable skills: Enhancing your research and employment potential*. Sage.

Dunleavy, Patrick, & Tinkler, Jane. (2021). *Maximizing the impacts of academic research: How to grow the recognition, influence, practical application and public understanding of science and scholarship*. Macmillan.

Eley, Adrian. R.; Wellington, Jerry; Pitts, Stephanie, & Biggs, Catherine. (2012). *Becoming a successful early career researcher*. Routledge. https://doi.org/10.4324/9780203113073

Habibie, Pejman, & Burgess, Sally (Eds.). (2021). *Scholarly publication trajectories of early-career scholars: Insider perspectives*. Palgrave Macmillan. https://doi.org/10.1007/978-3-030-85784-4

Jaeger, Audrey J., & Dinin, Alessandra J. (Eds.). (2018). *The postdoc landscape: The invisible scholars*. Academic Press. https://doi.org/10.1016/B978-0-12-813169-5.02001-2

Johnson, Alan M. (2011). *Charting a course for a successful research career: A guide for early career researchers*. (2nd ed.) Elsevier B.V.

Khoo, Tseen; Ward, Phil, & O'Donnell, Jonathan. (2023). *Getting research funded: Five essential rules for early career researchers*. Routledge.

Kwasnicka, Dominika, & Lai, Alden Yuanhong (Eds.). (2022). *Survival guide for early career researchers*. Springer.

Lemon, Narelle, & Salmons, Janette. (2021). *Reframing and rethinking collaboration in higher education and beyond: A practical guide for doctoral students and early career researchers*. Routledge.

Mahat, Marian, & Tatebe, Jennifer (Eds.). (2019). *Achieving academic promotion*. Emerald. https://doi.org/10.1108/9781787568990

McAlpine, Lynn, & Åkerlind, Gerlese. (2010). *Becoming an academic*. Palgrave Macmillan.

McAlpine, Lynn, & Amundsen, Cheryl. (2018). *Identity-trajectories of early career researchers: Unpacking the post-PhD experience*. Palgrave Macmillan. https://doi.org/10.1057/978-1-349-95287-8

Murgia, Annalisa, & Poggio, Barbara. (Eds.). (2019). *Gender and precarious research careers: A comparative analysis*. Routledge. https://doi.org/10.4324/9781315201245

Neave, Lucy; Connor, James, & Crawford, Amanda. (2007). *Arts of publication: Scholarly publishing in Australia and beyond*. Australian Scholarly Publishing.

Paltridge, Brian. (2017). *The discourse of peer review: Reviewing submissions to academic journals*. Springer. https://doi.org/10.1057/978-1-137-48736-0

Pommerening, Arne. (2021). *Staying on top in academia: A primer for (self-) mentoring young researchers in natural and life sciences*. Springer. https://doi.org/10.1007/978-3-030-65467-2

Roberts, Laura W., & Hilty, Donald M. (2017). *Handbook of career development in academic psychiatry and behavioral sciences*. (2nd ed.). American Psychiatric Association.

Roche, Joseph. (2022). *Essential skills or early career researchers*. Sage.

Singh, Jasvir Kaur Nachetar (Ed.). (2022). *Academic mobility and international academics: Challenges and opportunities*. Emerald. https://doi.org/10.1108/9781801175104

Spina, Nerida; Harris, Jess; Bailey, Simon, & Goff, Mhorag. (2020). *'Making it' as a contract researcher: A pragmatic look at precarious work*. Routledge.

Thwaites, Rachel, & Pressland, Amy (Eds.). (2017). *Being an early career feminist: Academic global perspectives, experiences and challenges*. Palgrave Macmillan. https://doi.org/10.1057/978-1-137-54325-7

Williams, Alison; Jones, Derek, & Robertson, Judy (Eds.). (2014). *BITE: Recipes for remarkable research*. Brill.

Zimmerman, Aaron Samuel. (2021). *Methodological innovations in research and academic writing*. IGI Global. https://doi.org/10.4018/978-1-7998-8283-1

Preparing for the ECR journey ahead

Overview

This chapter explains the key concepts underpinning the advice in this book's pointers and shows how these concepts can help design research careers around who you are and who you want to be. This chapter starts with your lived experiences as a thesis writer and the changes you might like to embark on in your career as an ECR. This chapter then introduces four ways of thinking about yourself to help you take control of who you are as an ECR researcher to plan your future career: ways of knowing, being, doing, and communicating (Figure 2.1).

Figure 2.1 The new 'you'.

DOI: 10.4324/9781003481034-2

Transitioning from thesis writer to ECR

To engage in the process of transitioning from a thesis writer to an ECR, this chapter starts by asking you to reflect on your past lived experiences so that you are in a better position to enact purposeful changes to move your career forward for you. There are no 'right' ways to proceed, just ones that are 'right' for you.

As an ECR, you are no longer a thesis writer yet those lived experiences have informed your ways of knowing, being, doing, and communicating. Some of these lived experiences will remain with you and guide your future career. Some associated ways of knowing, being, doing, and communicating you may want to change. Some of the changes may be subtle, others major. Some may be sudden, some gradual, some automatic. Many are conscious, but some are unconscious and can take years to fully understand.

Other major changes can involve entirely new forms of learning. Your thesis supervisors supervised you in a certain way. If you were unhappy with some of your lived experiences as a supervisee, you may want to develop other ways of doing supervision. You may have little other experience to draw on, and you may need to learn new ways of supervision. Deciding how you might create these new ways of doing can be daunting. For insights into supervision, see Chapter 7.

While you might be able to think through your ECR identity and any changes you want to make from your lived experiences as a thesis writer, sometimes knowing where to start can be difficult.

One natural starting place is your thesis. ECRs react differently to their lived experiences with their thesis. For some, the thesis will continue to have a major role in shaping and helping build their ECR career. If your lived experiences with your thesis continue to be a source of inspiration, your thesis and the ideas therein continue to energize you, you may want to spend the first part of your ECR career reworking parts of or perhaps all your thesis, for publication (see Pointer 12).

For others, you may have had enough of the thesis. The lived experiences of your thesis journey may be ones that you want to dissociate from (temporarily or permanently). You may need to refresh and take time off or do something different. You may travel and spend time with family, move on to a non-research position, or search out other research opportunities, related or unrelated to your thesis.

If you are looking for a new research direction, perhaps inspiration can be found in lived experiences from your thesis journey other than the thesis itself. Perhaps you attended a conference presentation about an interesting theoretical framework or methodology but were far too advanced in your thesis journey to consider it. Now might be your time to explore this new theory and/or methodology. Perhaps there are intriguing tidbits of knowledge in your data that you didn't explore because they didn't relate to the research questions posed in your thesis. Perhaps you might want to do something for your research community. During your thesis journey, you may have noted something in the community that you could help with, but you didn't have the time or energy to pursue it during your thesis journey. Now might be the time to reach out and offer your help.

Your thesis journey is another type of lived thesis experience that can be a source of inspiration. Perhaps you could write about the ways of being and doing that you acquired that helped you to complete your thesis. You have valuable lived experiences to share. Perhaps writing about your conflicts as a thesis writer and parent, a thesis writer in full-time employment, or a thesis writer working in their community can help in your own healing process while also helping those at the start of their thesis journey who might be feeling that they are alone in their conflicts.

Another way to forge ahead is to unpack different aspects of yourself during your thesis journey.

Your ways of knowing

Ways of knowing is a good place to start. Ways of knowing frame your ways of being, doing, and communicating, and are a good place to start thinking about the big picture of you. During your thesis journey, you homed in on different ways of knowing. Some of these ways of knowing were embedded into the content of your thesis. Others might have been fundamental to how you approached your thesis, or how you framed it. These ways of knowing informed how you wrote your thesis, and why you wrote it in the ways you did.

Some of these ways of knowing may have been personal ones; about the world in which you live; and how you process information around you on issues such as diversity and inclusion, non-Western ways of thinking, colonialism, climate change, environmental change, etc.

As an ECR, you are at a juncture in your life. Do you want your ways of knowing (i.e., about religion, gender, abortion, etc.) to become more overt in your ways of being and doing for your own wellbeing? Do you want some of your ways of knowing to be expressed more subtly (i.e., by your use of modifiers that temper ideas (i.e., 'possible' vs 'probable' rather than definitive statements)? Perhaps when interacting with some groups, individuals, or in some contexts, you may want your ways of knowing to be hidden entirely. You might do this by what is left unsaid (i.e., if you do not represent one side of an argument as a possibility, it can be inferred that you have little or no interest in a particular way of knowing or that you give it little credibility). There are different ways of knowing and you can bring yours to the fore in your own way.

Because you are at a natural juncture, there may be ways of knowing you want to change. If your ontological premises and epistemological ways of seeing the world have shifted since you completed your doctoral studies, you may want to search out new frameworks.

Any change in your ways of knowing affects your ways of doing. You might consider footnotes in your publications; explicit comments to your supervisees, or a statement on your social media platform to explain any change in your ways of knowing.

Your ways of being and doing

You are no longer a PhD candidate. You are an ECR. Some of your ways of being will continue as they did in your thesis journey. For example, you may work with the same research communities, in much the same way you did as a thesis writer. Your relationships with those communities may continue and change may not be significant. In other aspects, you are very different in your ways of doing. As examples, you are likely to have less regular contact with your supervisors and you may go to the campus where you completed your thesis less often, or not at all. You may spend more time in the publication game, writing more journal articles or book chapters. You may co-author with (more) people outside your supervision team and perhaps on topics that differ from your thesis topic. If you have decided that a research identity is not for you, your ways of doing are likely to shift in a completely different direction (see Pointer 49).

If you decide to pursue your research journey, you might now consider which of your ways of doing (observed and/or acquired while completing your thesis) are ones you want to bring with you into your early career research. Consider how these relate to your emerging and imagined ECR ways of being. You might reflect on your thesis journey and any ways of being that helped you in your thesis. Were you a confident researcher, a great networker, or a strong writer? If so, remember this and use those ways to move your research forward. Think about ways of doing that worked for you (i.e., you met deadlines, you were well-prepared for supervision meetings, you diligently worked through feedback). Hold on to these ways of doing as part of your ECR identity.

If some aspects of your doing during your thesis journey were not so great, now is a good time to think about change. In your thesis, what dragged you down and made you go off track? Could you meet the deadlines? Did you address every comment your supervisors made?

No one wants a co-author who doesn't meet deadlines, and who doesn't react at all, or well, to co-author comments. Now is the time to decide on new ways of doing that align with how you imagine yourself as an ECR, and enact change, if needed.

Your ways of communicating

One of your ways of doing as an ECR is as a communicator.

Writing is an integral part of work as an ECR, the more prepared you are for different ways of writing, the easier it will be for you to publish. If you wrote your thesis as a single monograph, you might need to change your writing style dramatically if you take a position in an industry where you will be writing research briefs and reports. If you want to remain in a university and develop your career as an academic, you will need to write journal articles, book chapters, or even a book. These may be types of writing you did not experience as a thesis writer. Increasingly, in any profession, you will use social media to introduce yourself and your research in your work context. As an ECR, what worked for you as a thesis writer may not work for you now. As you engage with different forms of communication, remind yourself that you can be a good writer in one genre, but you may still be an emerging one in another. Give yourself time to learn new ways of communicating.

Communication also involves knowing how to respond to feedback. Reflect on how you reacted to written or oral comments about your work in your thesis for inspiration. You might want to continue in ways that worked for you but possibly change some. Were your initial reactions to any feedback you received positive or negative? Did you use feedback to move an idea forward in novel ways that might have taken you some time and effort to implement? When you looked at feedback, did you look for the overall message being made before you read the details? Did you look at everything? It's easy to miss a critical point entirely. If you were unsure, did you ask for help with comments you found difficult to interpret? See Pointer 17.

As an ECR, you will be providing feedback to your colleagues, managers, students, supervisees, and research community. No one is perfect but some individuals might inspire you. You might want to sit in on classes run by lecturers with great teaching evaluations, observe good supervisors in interaction, and observe researchers in workshops. How do they show that they listen intently to what others are trying to tell them? When making these observations, think about how loudly they talk when disagreeing with a point, and how they use their body language to segment their ideas into manageable parts or stress the relative importance of certain points. We are all different, and while not all these ways of doing align with your ways of being and doing as an ECR, some will.

Communication is two-way. Think about how your comments are received by others (i.e., your co-author, supervisee, co-worker, manager, or students). You don't want to be known as a 'scary' supervisor, teacher, or employee/manager who only focuses on the negative or one who doesn't seem to want to understand the argument being developed. Impressions are not always formed by what is said or written, but rather by how it is said or written. Starting with the positive can help. Providing useful examples is also a helpful technique.

The following chapters in this book are in the form of pointers on topics and concerns of relevance to many ECRs. The advice in each pointer is built around individual ways of knowing, being, doing, and communicating, and is designed to help you better understand yourself as you move forward in your career. To understand yourself a little more, it helps to dream a little. Chapter 3 asks you to imagine your ideal future researcher identity.

Further reading

Browning, Thompson, and Dawson (2017) focus on how to get ahead as an ECR. They provide testimonials from established leading researchers on the importance of planning step-by-step progression. Chapman et al.

(2015) focus on research impact. While they draw on issues in the field of conservation research, many of their points have relevance to any social scientist working with communities. Kent et al. (2022) provide advice on empowerment for researchers in hard sciences but the advice given is equally useful in social sciences. Monereo and Liesa (2022) is a phenomenological study of five Early Career Researchers and a great read. They reveal the non-linear and non-hierarchical complexity of identity developments as individuals progress through thesis writing into ECR. Phillips et al. (2023) also consider how you want to position yourself in your research. Although the article is directed toward women, the basic questions discussed are useful for all researchers.

References

Browning, Lynette; Thompson, Kirrilly, & Dawson, Drew. (2017). From early career researcher to research leader: Survival of the fittest? *Journal of Higher Education and Policy Management, 39*(4), 361–377, https://doi.org/10.1080/1360080X.2017.1330814

Chapman, Jacqueline M.; Algera, Dirk; Dick, Melissa; Hawkins, Emily E. et al. (2015). Being relevant: Practical guidance for early career researchers interested in solving conservation problems. *Global Ecology and Conservation, 4*, 334–348, https://dx. doi.org/10.1016/j.gecco.2015.07.013

Kent, Brianne A.; Homan, Constance; Amoako, Emmanuella; Antonietti, Alberto et al. (2022). Recommendations for empowering early career researchers to improve research culture and practice. *PlosS Biol, 20*(7), e3001680, https://doi.org./10.1371/journal.pbio.3001680

Monereo, Charles, & Liesa, Eva. (2022). Early career researchers' identity positions based on research experiences. *Higher Education Research and Development, 41*(1), 193–210, https://doi.org/10.1080/07294360.2020.1835834

Phillips, Matthew J.; Dzidic, Peta L.; Roberts, Lynne D., & Castell, Emily L. (2023). "Comply, strategise, or resist?": Exploring early-career women's academic identities in Australian higher education using Foucauldian discourse analysis. *SN Social Sciences, 3*(81), 1–38, https://doi.org/10.1007/s43545-023-00668-w

Building your research career

Overview

This chapter introduces the first set of pointers in this book. They encourage you to put your ways of knowing, being, doing, and communicating at the forefront to set the stage for building your research career. The first pointer focuses on appreciating that every ECR is unique and that ECR journeys differ. This is vital for your wellbeing. The second pointer centers on your future: your imagined research career and the type of research you want to be known for. The aim here is to help you identify and develop a brand that can guide your research into a successful career. Later pointers in this chapter focus on ways to promote you and your brand through social media and conferences. The final pointers cover suggestions on preparing for your dream position and keeping yourself safe during your research (Figure 3.1).

Figure 3.1 No two ECRs are alike.

1. No two ECRs are alike

Not every ECR starts on the same level playing field. ECRs have different lived experiences during their thesis journey. Ask yourself: How have your prior experiences prepared you for research? During your thesis journey, have you published an article on your own? Have you successfully applied for grants? Have you supervised masters or honors students? If some of these ways of doing are new to you it may take time to understand how best to do them. It's important not to concentrate on what other ECRs are achieving. They may have had a head start.

Another obvious difference between ECRs is their employment status. Some ECRs are lucky enough to have secured full time research positions within a university setting with access to scholars (i.e, experienced co-authors, mentors), resources (i.e., research assistants, interns, computer programs, internal grants, etc.), and specialized professional development (i.e., grant writing). Some positions come with more resources than others. There are also other differences. If you have a full time research position, it may not be the same as one in another institution. Research positions come with different amounts of research time (from 100% to 10%) and institutions count research differently. Some institutions count supervision under research, others do not. At times, institutions place their emphasis on other forms of research. Some institutions place more emphasis on grant writing, others on grant success (see Pointer 11 on institutional foci). Each situation sets you at a different starting point on your ECR career path.

There are other differences. If you work in industry, have a government position, or are employed in the private sector, your employment status can constrict what you publish, when, and how. Your research may need to be published in the name of the company, government department, or NGO. Some grants from private enterprises may have a temporary (and sometimes permanent) moratorium on publication. If your employment obligations restrict the nature of your research output, it will take longer to publish than if you were to research on your terms.

Many ECRs are reading the above paragraph thinking these are luxuries you do not have. If you have a full time teaching-only position, rely on contract work, work in hospitality, or are unemployed, you have limited time and resources for research. It will take you longer to achieve research outputs, but it needn't determine what you can achieve.

Another obvious difference between the amount of research you can expect to produce relates to the nature of the research. Some research takes longer to complete. An ECR conducting anonymous online surveys will take less time to conduct their research than an ECR working in communities. If you are drawing on research from existing databases, you have a head start over ECRs who are collecting new data. If your research involves deep philosophical work, it can be very time consuming to complete. Longitudinal research won't achieve immediate outcomes.

Other differences stem from individual ways of being and doing. Some ECRs work as part of a team, others work alone. Co-researching with established researchers can produce more outcomes than if you work alone but you can get where you want to be as a solo author.

Work habits also differ. Some researchers can manage multiple projects; others need to work on one project at a time. It is best to work in ways that are authentic to you for your long term health and wellbeing.

Risk-taking is another point of difference that can accelerate some careers. Some ECRs have an appetite for risk-taking; others do not. Some ECRs are prepared to submit journal articles and grants or apply for positions; other ECRs may not yet feel that the work is ready and delay submissions. Although risk-taking might be quicker, it is not necessarily the healthiest option for everyone. It's good to take chances but you need to keep your wellbeing in mind.

Life outside of research is another difference. Some ECRs are focused only on their career. Others care for family, juggle multiple forms of employment, need selfcare, or want to enjoy having weekends and evenings to pursue personal adventures and pastimes. If this is you, it doesn't mean that you can't do research or have an early research career, it just means that you may not be able to produce as many research outputs as an ECR with less going on in their life. Setting achievable goals allows you to reach your objectives and achieve a work-life balance that suits you.

The key message here is to think about what you can and want to do at the beginning of your career. Others might provide you with ideas, and stimuli, but they aren't you. It's important to work at your own pace and agenda. You have a whole life ahead of you. You don't want to burn yourself out in the first few years or dwell on the achievements of other ECRs.

Further reading

Chapter 2 in Macaulay (2023) focuses on identity development within a university context. He highlights the influence of institutional norms and practices on ECRs, and the risk of losing 'you' within the narrative of career success.

Reference

Macaulay, Luke (2023). Entering a career as an ECR in an increasingly shifting academic landscape: The value of different forms of capital. In Basil Cahusac de Caux, Lynette Pretorius & Luke Macaulay (Eds.), *Research and teaching in a pandemic world: The challenges of establishing academic identities during times of crisis*, pp. 327–342. Springer Nature. https://doi.org/10.1007/978-981-19-7757-2

2. What's your brand?

To get where you want to be, it helps to build a narrative about who you are, what you do, and how you want to engage with others in research. This narrative work is all about branding. Branding helps move your career forward in coherent ways. It makes it easier to promote yourself and your research and stay on track in your ECR journey.

To begin, ask yourself about your imagined future research. Do you want to continue in the same direction (if so how), or would you like to move on to something else? If you have never really known who you are as an ECR, feel that your research interests are scattered all over the place, and have difficulty defining your research, now is the time to look for a clearer focus. Finetuning your brand can take time. It's okay to think for a while about where you want your research to take you. It's also okay to change your mind.

Defining and articulating your brand is not an easy task. Research is often complex and intertwined. It might help if you start with your thesis. Why did you choose your thesis topic? How does your thesis topic relate to other work you have published or are currently working on? Some connections may be tenuous, but they are connections all the same. The connections might be theoretical, they may involve methodologies, datasets, or communities, or those connections might be centered around multiple interconnected research questions. Once you have some ideas, ask yourself if this research agenda makes you happy and is one that you want as the focus of your work for many years to come. You will know when you find it.

Your thinking should be somewhat broad in scope. You want a research direction to develop and for others to potentially contribute to (see Pointer 7 on co-authoring and Chapter 7 on supervising). However, you also don't want your brand to be so vague that your research lacks focus. The extent to which you narrow the focus of your brand is individual. If you like to ask many questions about a single phenomenon, you might be content with a very general brand to cover the narrative around your research (i.e., well-being). If you like working on small bits until you understand every small detail, it can help to have a brand that is narrower in focus (i.e., the wellbeing of GenZ women working in IT).

After you have a brand, the next step is to stay true to it and embed it in every aspect of your research life: This includes embedding it into your social network profiles (Pointer 3), conference presentations (Pointer 4), publications (Chapter 5), and grant applications (Chapter 6).

Your graduate research candidates also play a role in your brand. Their thesis titles and/or topics are often listed on your institutional research profile. Before accepting a research candidate, brainstorm how their proposed topic fits your brand. If a research candidate wants to work with you, they usually like something in what you are doing (see Pointer 31) and it doesn't hurt to see if they might be willing to tweak their ideas a little, or even a lot to fit with your current research. They might like your suggestions. It also doesn't hurt if your research candidates do something slightly different. If they think a little differently about your research topic, it could take your thinking about your research in a productive direction.

Some techniques can keep you focused on your brand. Consider composing a planning paragraph for each new publication or grant application. This might include details about why the topic of the envisaged work is important to you; how previous work (yours and others) has helped build your interest in this topic; the gaps in this research area that need to be filled (and why); and which one you are focusing on now. This type of brainstorming paragraph helps maintain focus (and decide whether the publication or grant is a good idea for your brand before you start to write it). If you are not keen on planning paragraphs, a template of questions could achieve the same purpose.

Branding is not fixed for life. Your brand will narrow, broaden, and can even change in major ways as you progress in your thinking and your ECR career. The important thing is that you recognize when you are deviating from your research direction (and how) so that you can make decisions about whether the change is good for you and your career development. Moving from one position to another often gives you opportunities to adjust your research direction. How does what you want to do next fit with what you have done in the past? Your narrative will have different chapters over time. We rarely ever start completely anew.

Further reading

Bentley et al. (2019) explore professional identity construction during the doctoral journey. The article explains how multiple identities help support identity transitions from the past, present, and into an imagined future. It can be an equally useful read for ECRs. Lieff et al. (2012) discuss how academic identity is formed and developed as a dynamic construct. Their field of research is Allied Health, but their observations apply much more broadly.

References

Bentley, Sarah V.; Peters, Kim; Haslam, S. Alexander, & Greenaway, Katherine H. (2019). Construction at work: Multiple identities scaffold professional identity development in academia. *Frontiers in Psychology, 10*(628), 1–10, https://doi.org/10.3389/fpsyg.2019.0062

Lieff, Susan; Baker, Lindsay; Mori, Brenda; Egan-Lee, Eileen, et al. (2012). Who am I? Key influences on the formation of academic identity within a faculty development program. *Medical Teacher, 34*(3), e208–e215, https://doi.org/10.3109/0142159X.2012.642827

3. What's your social media strategy?

Publicizing you and your brand is important to a successful ECR career. If you keep a low profile, few researchers will know about your work. Social media gets your research out there. A well-considered social media plan increases both your academic visibility and research impact (see Pointer 13 on research impact).

Sometimes social media can produce instant results. Some social media platforms allow you to post a conference paper you have just presented. You can post a picture of yourself at the conference, or in the field. You can circulate the DOI of your latest publication. Should your post be shared by an influential person, it may do wonders for promoting you and your work. Put simply, social media supports you by advertising your name, face, and research to the wider research community. This helps others discover you and your research.

There is a lot of choice. Different platforms and Apps have different audiences and offer differing formats for disseminating your research. Your institutional profile is an important social media tool as it helps people find you. Make completing your institutional profile a priority. Fellow researchers might want you to work on a research grant, write a chapter in an edited volume, or review an article in your field of expertise, if they can find you. Good potential graduate candidates want to know about your research interests, publications, previous supervision, teaching expertise, and research expertise before they enquire about your availability to supervise them.

Because institutional profiles have a stipulated format, order, and prescribe certain types of content, they may not reflect all your ways of being and doing as you might like them. You may want to use another platform. Or perhaps you don't yet have a secure position. There are other social platforms to promote you and your work. The first step is deciding which platforms and Apps serve your purposes best.

You might consider uploading your details on a general social network site for research professionals (i.e., LinkedIn, ResearchGate, and Google Scholar). These sites work differently from your institutional profile. They ask you to upload information about yourself and your publications and use this information to help build a following through their algorithms. The algorithms enable you to follow researchers in your own and other fields and keep you up to date with new work. Some enable you access to yet-to-be-published work.

These sorts of professional social network sites can provide valuable support if you are unemployed, working in a remote location, or working in another location where there are few like-minded researchers in the immediate vicinity. These platforms also use your publications to produce data on your 'research impact', such as downloads, reads, shares, and citations, all of which are useful for your CV (see Pointer 44).

There are other options. Some professional associations allow you to use their networks to advertise you and your work. You can also use these sites to passively monitor what others are doing. This might include notifications from researchers engaging in projects similar to yours. Such information helps you locate potential research collaborators and co-authors and stay connected through upcoming conferences.

Other more general social media platforms such as Facebook groups have different purposes. They are a great way to reach out to diverse groups to promote a project. You might crowdsource participants or use the platform as a forum to explore ideas with a wide audience. Although many ideas in the comments provide few insights, there may be a gem among them. Perhaps one of the ideas could turn your research in a more productive direction, saving you time and money.

If a more informal media appeals to you, blogging might be your thing. Platforms with blog pages offer opportunities for you to publish in informal ways through written commentary, videos, images, and audio content. Platforms such as YouTube allow you to create content in a format and length that suits most purposes. This offers excellent opportunities to promote your research to a wider audience.[1] For a winning formula, keep the content simple and explain yourself as if you were giving an introductory lecture to a group of students with no background in the field. It helps to keep the content short and your point interesting enough to keep your audience watching. You can tell jokes!

If short and sharp suits your ways of communicating, microblogging Apps abound. Short-form limited character or video length formats like X or TikTok have multiple uses. They are great for publicizing your work, staying current with newly published material, or seeking advice on general research issues such as equipment and methodologies.

Ultimately, the type of social media you access depends on you and how you like to work. If using social media is deeply embedded in your ways of being and doing, having multiple social network platforms can be a form of relaxation and monitoring them can be fun. If social networking is important to your ways of communicating, think strategically about how to maximize benefits but limit the time spent, that is, you can monitor your profiles in your off time while you travel on public transport, or while waiting in your office for your next meeting. If you get caught up monitoring media sites for long periods, monitor when and how you use social media, and try to allocate some of the time you spend on social media to work on a grant or publication or to read the latest piece of work your doctoral candidate has sent you. If social media is getting in the way of quality time with friends and family, now and then you might consider leaving your phone at home when you go out.

For some ECRs, it isn't too great of a social media presence that is the issue but rather not having enough of one. If you are an ECR who finds social media a largely scary world difficult to navigate, you may find monitoring and updating social media stressful and tedious. If this is the case, restrict the number of platforms you sign up to as it will do your health and wellbeing little good to have to monitor them. If you are lucky to work in a research institution, tech help is readily available to finetune your profile or link platforms, so you only have to check in one place.

Further reading

Lemon (2014) writes about her experiences of being a woman in academia and how she found social networking a valuable way of reaching out to other ECRs to explore ideas. Zhu and Procter (2015) present a general guide on potential uses of social media by PhD students. This work is useful for ECRs who have limited experience utilizing social media in their research careers.

References

Lemon, Narelle. (2014). Sending out a Tweet: Finding new ways to network in academia. In Narelle Lemon & Suzanne Garvis (Eds.), *Being "In and out": Providing voice to early career women in academia*, pp. 43–54. Springer.

Zhu, Yimei, & Procter, Rob. (2015). Use of blogs, Twitter and Facebook by UK PhD students for scholarly communication. *Observatorio*, 9(2), 29–46.

4. Using conferences to promote your brand

While social media networks are a relatively new way of increasing visibility in your research community (see Pointer 3), conferences are a well-established strategy. Conferences gather people of similar interests in a location, where they can present and discuss topics of common interest, engage in social networking opportunities, apply for jobs, and even attend interviews. With conferences in differing formats and sizes, there is much to choose from, and you need to be selective. This pointer considers the available options and how you can get the most out of the conference experience.

While you can attend the conference purely for networking and learning about current work in the field, if you aim to promote your brand, you need to present a conference paper. There are three basic types of conference papers. First, you can present a conference paper that promotes completed work. This type of conference paper enables you to publicize upcoming publications. Alternatively, you may want to present a conference paper on work that you feel needs some refinement. Conference papers are great for organizing thoughts and consolidating ideas so that you can streamline your research and turn it into a journal article or book chapter.[2] A third possibility is to present a conference paper to unpack a very new research idea. If this is your preference, inform your audience of your intentions and keep your paper well under the time limit to allow lots of time for questions and feedback.

When considering presenting at a conference, you might be tempted to present more than one paper. This may not be your best option. If you are presenting multiple papers, you have less time to focus on crafting each work, you won't have as much time to enjoy the conference, and you diminish your time for networking. If you have more than one paper that you could present, select the paper with the broadest appeal. A conference paper with a wider appeal will usually get better attendance and a better timeslot.[3]

A second issue is which conference to choose. Selecting the most appropriate conference is not always easy. While you need a conference that you can benefit from, conferences come in many formats, with some a better fit for you than others.

Smaller in-person conferences and workshops have built into them longer breaks between sessions and longer lunches. These provide more opportunities to talk informally with researchers you haven't met before; who you know but would like to get to know better; and those you know well but haven't seen for a while. In other words, small conferences give ample opportunities to network socially and showcase who you are and what you do.

Informal interactions of this kind have potential long term benefits: new contacts might offer you mentoring, serve as potential reviewers for your grants, or become a potential co-author. While such opportunities exist in larger forums, the more intimate contexts provided through smaller conferences usually produce more such opportunities.

Larger in-person international conferences offer opportunities of a different kind. They are great places to observe big names in the field, keep abreast of upcoming ideas pre-publication, or explore future employment. Bigger conferences have some downsides. They come with larger crowds and some ECRs can find this overwhelming. If large crowds unnerve you, think about having a co-author to co-present and keep you company to help improve your conference experience. You might also want to seek out a conference that offers a 'buddy' system where experienced conference attendees buddy up with a newbie. Some conferences have special events for ECRs that can make you feel welcome and not lost in the crowds.

At larger conferences, if there are researchers you would like to meet, email them before the conference to arrange a time to meet. It's hard to find people at the spur of the moment with such large crowds.

Online conferences are another option for those of you who are time poor, shy, and/or tech-savvy. They provide you with outlets to publicize your work and hear new ideas in the field, and they are often less expensive (an important consideration for many). They are also good for making connections. You can connect with like-minded researchers by sending them a message immediately after their presentation.

While most ECRs know about conferences, workshops, and seminars in their fields of expertise, there are further opportunities outside your field. Attending conferences outside your field can provide you with new ideas about how you might apply your existing work to a different context. New ideas and differing applications of existing ones help craft later publications in ways that get the attention of editors as they enhance the perceived value of your research and offer you a richer range of publication outlets (and potential grant avenues).

While it may be helpful to know about the different conferences out there, you can't go to all the conferences you would like. You have neither the time nor the money. Before you decide to attend a conference, consider the costs involved, what expenses your place of employment might cover, and if working in a casual position, whether the conference offers subsidies for those in casual or part-time work. Look at the registration fees as mega international conferences have large registration fees. If you are short of cash, email the conference organizer and ask if you could assist at the conference in return for a reduced conference registration fee.

Another major expense is conference accommodation. Look out for conferences close to friends and family as this can reduce accommodation costs. Sometimes conferences offer email lists to send messages about accommodation. There may be another ECR who wants to share a hotel room, or one who lives locally and might have a spare room.

Another way to cut costs is to think about what else you could do on location. If you are attending an international conference, you might stay a couple of extra days and check out local institutions (or even libraries) for resources and opportunities. Or you might use that time to rework your conference paper into a journal article. It's amazing what you can achieve away from work and personal responsibilities. Alternatively, you might want to take a short holiday, hang out with new or old friends, and refresh mentally before you return to work.

If you are considering combining the conference with a family vacation, some conferences are family-friendly, with activities for family members, and limited childcare. Keep in mind that bringing family to the conference can be challenging, so consider whether this would work for you before committing yourself. It might be better to ask your family to join you for a few days after the conference concludes. That way you can have the best of both worlds.

Further reading

Becker (2014) is a useful guide on presenting conference papers. The final chapter in her book provides ideas about how to derive the best overall value from conference experiences.

Reference

Becker, Lucinda. (2014). *Presenting your research: Conferences, symposiums, poster presentations and beyond*. Sage.

5. What do you imagine 'success' to be?

Building your career means working to get where you want it and you to be. It also means thinking long term about your ideal position. It's easy to lose track of time and not get where you had planned to be in your career.

So perhaps it is time to daydream about the best location to achieve your research goals, and how you might get there. Where is exciting work being done in your field? It might be in another city or another country. Consider what you would need if you wanted a position in this location. It helps to think laterally. Would you benefit from enrolling in a short English language teaching course (i.e., CELTA or IELTS) to help you teach in a country where English is not the official language? Or perhaps it would be useful to enrol in a foreign language class. Even if English is the workplace language, it helps to know a little of the local language. Perhaps there are other endeavors (i.e., gaining more teaching or supervision experience) that could help you work toward your ideal position.

Sometimes the best way to achieve your ideal position is to start with research links. Perhaps you might consider collaborating on research grants between your current workplace and where you would ideally like to work. Or it is strategic to secure co-authored publications with researchers in your ideal work location. If so, think about how many, and what types of publications would make a difference to your success. (See Chapter 5 on publications for further information.)

Perhaps there is a need for another sort of daydreaming – one that focuses on the preferred institution where you would like to work (abroad or in your current place of residence). Different achievements count as success in differing types of employment contexts. If your ideal job is in government, smaller technical reports might do you well. If your perfect job is in a teaching college, a few minor publications and good teaching evaluations might be what you need. If your ideal job is at a major university, then spending time on securing a strong publication in the best journal in your field might work for you. If you work for a research institute, external grants may be what you need for your CV.

If there is a team of scholars at a location that you would like to work with, contacting those researchers before you apply for a job might increase your chances of getting the desired position. It might also inform you if these researchers are ones who you would like to work with. Any transition into a new workplace is easier if contacts are set up beforehand.

While all this dreaming is important, be prepared for the costs. Moving creates temporary havoc in your life: professional, financial, and emotional. Packing, locating accommodation, and setting up your home (and your office) can take a month or two away from valuable research. It may take up to a year to truly settle into a new life and work routine. This takes away continuity of thought and can wreak havoc on the careers of those ECRs who like fixed routines.

There will never be a perfect time to move. If life is messier than normal, apply for the position all the same, and if you get the position, negotiate if you can delay taking up the position. Most new places of employment try to accommodate your needs if you explain your circumstances. It helps to be open with employers.

Further reading

A short article by Crase (1993) gives insights into many characteristics of highly productive scholars. Although the article was written decades ago, much of the content is relevant today. For a look at how research needs to adapt and be flexible, we recommend McArdle (2022).

References

Crase, Darrell. (1993). Highly productive scholars: What drives them to success? *Journal of Physical Education, Recreation & Dance*, 64(6), 80–82.

McArdle, Rachel. (2022). Flexible methodologies: A case for approaching research with fluidity. *The Professional Geographer*, 74(4), 620–627, https://doi.org/10.1080/00330124.2021.2023593

6. Taking care of yourself in research

Whatever your position, it is good to be reminded of potential perils in your workplace (and how to avoid them). Research activity can sometimes throw unexpected curveballs that have the potential to impact your physical and mental wellbeing.

Safety is a consideration in any workplace. If you tripped or had an accident in the carpark, could you get help? If you slipped while working in your office at night, would you be able to get assistance? Do you have a handy list of emergency numbers to carry with you?

If your research involves interacting with others, there are other safety concerns. Is there any possibility that you could put yourself in harm's way by researching on location? When conducting research, are you meeting in a safe place and time of day? If you are unsure, is there someone there you trust? Could you take another researcher or a research assistant with you?

Another safety concern involves what you are told or see. When you interview people, run a focus group, or even elicit material online, you can be surprised (even shocked) by what you encounter. Ethics processes ask you to consider most eventualities to ensure that you plan for your safety and the safety of your participants. If you are conducting research into obvious sensitive issues (i.e., sexual abuse, poverty, or rescued animals), you are likely to have had training for such eventualities. Yet unexpected situations can happen. You may be happily interviewing a participant about something mundane (i.e., their shopping experiences in the local precinct) when they reveal that they witnessed a robbery. In some cases, your participant may give you information about an illegal activity, and you may have a duty to report it to the police. If your research involves interacting with people, before you go into the field, seek training where available, and get advice from anyone you can. This might be an experienced researcher or your mentor. Discussing all potential eventualities will be time well spent.

In some cases, traumatic events may take another form. If you have experienced a past trauma in your personal or academic life, is there any chance that you could encounter hearing or seeing a similar event in your research that might affect you? While you may be able to repress a memory at that moment, trauma may reemerge later in unexpected ways. If you have experienced a past trauma in your life, what safeguards do you need to put in place? Who can you talk to and debrief? Only you have the answers. If unsure, contact a member of the ethics committee for help. You may be surprised by the similarities between your needs and other researchers. They have access to counselling services and can put you in touch with appropriate services. Ask for help if and when you need it.

You also need to keep safe your online presence. Be selective and careful in what you post. To avoid misappropriation and/or the misuse of your research and data, you need to protect them. Check if your institution has any requirements or protocols for safeguarding the security of your data, sensitive material, and records. Always exercise caution with any new platforms. You also need to ensure that you have measures in place to protect yourself. If your work is controversial, you may lose privacy; or worse, you can be subject to trolling and online witch hunts. To mitigate any and all risks, ask for technical support if you are the least bit unsure.

Finally, there are instances during your research journey where your personal life needs time to heal (i.e., death of a loved one, separation or divorce, serious illness, or even accidents). Your physical and emotional health underpins your research. Take care of yourself first.

Further reading

Baccarella et al. (2018) summarize the benefits and pitfalls of publishing research online. Kumar and Cavallaro (2018) developed a conceptual framework for selfcare in emotionally demanding research. They draw on their experiences conducting research in sensitive fields related directly to their lives.

References

Baccarella, Christian V.; Wagner, Timm F.; Kietzman, Jan H., & McCarthy, Ian P. (2018). Understanding the dark side of social media. *European Management Journal, 36*(4), 431–438, https://doi.org/10.1016/j.emj.2018.07.002

Kumar, Smita, & Cavallaro, Liz. (2018). Researcher self-care in emotionally demanding research: A proposed conceptual framework. *Qualitative Health Research, 28*(4), 648–658, https://doi.org/10.1177/1049732317746377

Notes

1 Although many YouTube videos put your face in public, you don't need to design your video this way. You can create your platform using drawings, a PowerPoint presentation or a series of narrated pictures.
2 If you are presenting a conference paper that you are trying to write up for publication, listen carefully at question time. If your ideas are not sufficiently focused, it will become obvious from the questions the audience ask (i.e., Are you trying to say …).
3 Timeslots are important at conferences. If you are allocated a slot with limited appeal (i.e., the first slot in the morning after the conference dinner or the last slot of the conference), contact the organizers and ask if a change is possible if someone pulls out and another slot becomes available. Do this as early as possible.

 # Collaborations

Overview

Success might be a solitary experience, but with every lived experience there is often someone who has helped you along the way. The pointers in this chapter look at collaborations that can help build your career. The first pointer considers an important and growing form of collaboration: co-authoring and what to search for in a good co-author. Subsequent pointers look to the benefits of mentors and support networks in your research journey and two somewhat unusual forms of collaboration: the potential of committee membership in assisting and supporting you and your research and how to benefit from aligning your research with institutional branding (Figure 4.1).

Figure 4.1 Collaborating will help you progress.

7. Co-authoring

Co-authoring for career success: it builds and extends your brand establishing new ways of doing. It provides new insights and opportunities for greater research impact. You enhance your research journey through new friendships, and you may get to laugh a little. Laughing is good for your wellbeing.

Importantly, a co-author helps get research done. You can split the work, and bounce ideas off one another and move them forward in useful directions. A co-author can question ideas and the premises behind them before you go too far down a track that leads nowhere.

When individuals work well together, the research outcomes are speedier and stronger.

There are different reasons for co-authoring. A mutual interest in the topic is critical. If you know you work well together, that is even better. If your thesis experience was enjoyable, one or more of your supervisors might make for good co-authors. They know how you work and wouldn't have supervised you if they didn't have a particular interest in at least one part of your thesis. Perhaps you know other researchers working with theories, methodologies, or data who you think would be good to work with. You may have met someone at a conference (see Pointer 4), listened to their paper and hit it off.

Research interests don't need to be identical, co-authoring with researchers with different ways of doing and knowing can help extend your research into new areas. Your co-author may be someone in a different field, adding quite different perspectives. A co-author could be someone with an interesting dataset that you can use to pose a research question close to your heart. Take time to talk to colleagues, you may discover complementary interests.

A mutual commitment to complete the work is necessary for co-authoring. If a potential co-author is too busy and somewhat reluctant to take on new projects, you should find someone else (at least for now). An unsuitable co-author can create chaos in your life and your publication plan.

Compatibility in ways of working is equally important. If potential co-authors are known to work at a pace that is too slow or fast (i.e., they return work within 24 hours and you don't want to work to that schedule, or you want a speedy response and they often take months before they get back to you), this can lead to endless stress. Have discussions about turnaround times before you commit. No one will match perfectly but you want to start with the best possible match.

You might also research writing styles before you decide to co-author. Read something your potential co-author(s) have written and think about whether you write in ways that are similar or ways that appeal to you. Conflicting writing styles make it difficult to construct coherent text and can take valuable time away from other research activities.

When deciding who should write what, you need to know what you and your co-author do well. You might be good at organizing ideas and locating relevant literature. There are things you do well but don't particularly enjoy. You may be good at transcription but find it excruciatingly tedious. Referencing might drive you crazy. Your co-author might take great joy in those parts of the research journey, and this division of labour will benefit you both. When everyone knows how to work together, what they can each contribute, and what to expect from each other the work gets done.

Strengths may emerge partway through a project. Some researchers are better at responding to disappointing or crushing reviews, especially if a rethink or rewrite is required. Co-authoring is an ongoing learning experience, and you may need to revisit discussions about strengths/weaknesses and likes/dislikes throughout your partnership

If considering a major project with multiple researchers, start small. A small project lets you know how well you work together before you commit to a larger project that might last several years. Prior co-authored research lets funding agencies know that as a team you can successfully work together (see Pointer 20).

Finally, if you work in a university setting, there are guidelines about preferred types of authorship. In some cases, universities, faculties, and disciplines prefer sole-authored works, at other times they prefer co-authorship. Considering how your forms of authorship fit within your institutional setting (see Pointer 11 for further details) is important for career success and can affect how many single-authored or co-authored works you may want to have in your publication plan.

Further reading

Durkin (1992) is a short article. It is an older piece but is still a useful checklist if you are considering whether single or co-authoring is the best option for you right now. Eodice and Day's (2003) full-length free-access book is a great resource for those wanting details about the personal experiences of co-authoring.

References

Durkin, Mick. (1992). Some dynamics of authorship. *Australia Universities Review,* 35(1), 43–48.

Eodice, Michele, & Day, Kami. (2003). *First person squared: A study of co-authoring in the academy.* Utah State University Press. *Project MUSE* muse.jhu.edu/book/9351

8. Mentors

Learning is lifelong and creating a successful career often means learning and leaning on others. A good mentor can help you navigate your ECR journey and offer novel ways of thinking around issues that are slowing your research or getting you down. A good mentor is like a good friend – invaluable.

Mentors offer different types of support. You may want a mentor who guides you in your career development (i.e., how to create research opportunities, timely promotions, and build your career path). The rules for career progression can be complex and it helps to have someone experienced to guide you. Or a mentor who gives tips on writing that can increase your chances of a successful publication or successful grant application. A writing mentor can point out serious gaps in your argument or point to a way of making your argument stronger. Other types of mentors help you manage stress, offer advice about where to go if you are having a career meltdown, and support you to develop your confidence as a successful researcher or supervisor. In other words, mentors have different strengths, and it can be good to have more than one mentor.

As you consider mentors, think carefully about your ways of being and doing and how you might ensure you find a mentor who understands you. To get the most out of a mentor-mentee relationship, you need honest conversations about the advice you want and what a potential mentor is comfortable providing. Good mentor-mentee relationships are built on trust. You need to be willing to say what you think, know that you are being heard and be confident that conversations remain confidential.

Another important consideration is you and your mentor's ways of being and doing. If you are an ECR who likes informal ways of being and doing, think about a mentor who suits those ways of doing. The better the fit, the more valuable the relationship. You are unlikely to find a perfect match, but you do want someone you can talk with easily. A few questions you might ask yourself include: Do you work best when you are supported by someone who is endlessly positive? Are you an ECR who prefers sugar-coated advice or advice that is blunt and to the point? Do you want someone to push you forward in a particular direction or someone who gives you timely warnings of perils ahead but lets you make your own path forward? Do you need someone you can talk to without much notice or someone who likes to meet regularly at a certain time each week or month? Do you need a mentor who is overly familiar with your topic, or a mentor outside your field who asks questions and forces you to explain yourself better? The more you know about what you need and how you work, the more informed your choices will be. To start on the right track, before you approach someone to be your mentor, take a little time to get to know them and decide whether you can work well together.

Once you know the kind of mentor you want, you need to find them. That person need not be someone new. If someone from your previous contacts gave you advice and support and they suited your ways of being and doing, consider approaching them to ask if they would be receptive to a mentorship relationship. If one of your supervisors was particularly helpful in offering help, you may ask if they want to continue to act in this capacity. There may have been other lecturers and tutors or the chair of your panel in your doctoral program who showed an interest in your PhD research and were supportive in ways you appreciated. Maybe they might make a good mentor. If you met a researcher at a conference you attended who took a keen interest in your work and its progress, you might ask them. There are lots of options. Perhaps you are currently collaborating on a project with an experienced researcher who could be a potential mentor. Perhaps there is someone you are working with on an academic committee (see Pointer 10 on joining committees), or perhaps someone you are co-supervising with.

The location of the mentor is important. A potential mentor from your current work context is likely to be more readily available to meet with you on short notice than someone outside your workplace. A mentor who works outside your work context is a better alternative if you want to discuss workplace issues. If you seek someone who understands work in your field from outside your workplace, you might look to mentors from your professional networks. If you are considering a future change in career direction finding a mentor who works in that area can be useful.

If you are uncomfortable raising the issue of mentorship because you don't want to impose on others' work time, formalized mentor programs work for you. Many institutions have formal mentoring programs. These may be a mandatory part of your workplace induction or a voluntary mentorship program. Sometimes, the mentors in these programs are great. They can offer increased belonging and attachment to the institution and help in career development. However, you might not get a great match. If mentorship arrangements are not working for you, ask your mentor if they wouldn't mind changing what is covered, or if you can meet less frequently. If you think another mentor would be better for you, you could approach the leadership and ask to change or opt out. Mentorship programs don't suit every ECR. If this form of collaboration doesn't work for you, you are wasting your time and that of your mentor.

After you gain more experience, you might like to consider how you can mentor ECRs who are less advanced in their careers, including any graduate researchers you supervise.

Further reading

We recommend Fenton, Walsh, and MacDonald's chapter on co-mentoring. This work describes the personal experience of a formalized mentor-mentee relationship developed through a national government research initiative. They discuss benefits such as greater publication output and confidence building. Schriever and Grainger (2019) provide insights into the perspectives of both mentors and mentees.

References

Fenton, Angela; Walsh, Kerryann, & MacDonald, Amy. (2016). Capacity building of early career researchers through cross-institutional mentoring. In. B. Gloria Guzman Johannessen (Ed.), *Global co-mentoring networks in higher education: Politics, policies, and practices*, pp. 203–227. Springer. http://doi.org/10.1007/978-3-319-27508-6

Schriever, Vicki, & Grainger, Peter. (2019). Mentoring an early career researcher: Insider perspectives from the mentee and mentor. *Reflective Practice, 20*(6), 720–731, https://doi.org/10.1080/14623943.2019.1674272

9. Developing support networks

Collaborations can involve groups of professionals. Professional and academic support networks can help you as you navigate your career. They can give you increased advice, increase your visibility within the field and make connections. Research careers can be lonely.

Participating in professional and academic networks builds your career in other ways. It demonstrates to workplaces a sense of collegiality, an interest in teamwork, the potential of entrepreneurship, and other highly prized qualities that you can only get by interacting with others in your field. Networks often have small grants that members can use to support their research.

The diversity of professional and academic networks out there means that you are sure to find one that is right for you.

Networks vary in size and purpose. Some networks are disciplinary, others interdisciplinary. Some are within your research institution, and some within your professional organizations. All networks are full of researchers who want to share ideas and talk about research, share insights about upcoming jobs, and offer advice from how to write grants and manuscripts to how best to structure your CV (see Pointer 44) or get promoted (see Pointer 48). They also offer emotional support, providing a forum to share small and large celebrations of success and commiserate disappointments with those who feel your pain.

Some professional, academic, and institutional networks cater to specific groups (i.e., women writers, part-time researchers, academics with young families, etc.). These groups establish contact with like-minded souls. For example, if you are a researcher with a young family or are Indigenous, you might seek out networks of like-minded researchers (or they may even seek you out). Smaller networks tend to have in-person meetings and opportunities to blend social and professional activities. Some meetings might be in the form of lunches, and others, writing circles.

You might want to explore multidisciplinary networks. These can be fun. These tend to offer similar support to field-specific networks but without field specifics. You learn about new and sometimes exciting or exotic things when you meet up with researchers from different fields to discuss theories and methodologies. These networks can open your thinking about wider applications for your work. They also help refine ways of communicating. The more you talk about what you do and why, the better you become at communicating who you are and who you want to be.

Field-specific networks can be large and global. These keep you current with upcoming research and provide information on grants, job opportunities, conferences, seminars, etc. (see Pointer 3 on social media). These networks are often online but may meet up once a year at an annual conference.

These network events are helpful when you don't know many people at a conference (see Pointer 4).

Some networks operate exclusively online, some mostly online but with regular events that offer in-person meetings. These are great when you live in less accessible locations, are time restricted, or are a little shy about face-to-face meetings with researchers you don't know well. If it's an online format, choose one that suits you. Some networks work through emails, others through asynchronous or synchronous websites.

If you are seeking a network but not finding something that suits your needs, ask other scholars in your field or department, your former supervisors or even ask around at your next conference. Watch workplace newsletters for mentions of networks and ask your school or department head.

If you are entrepreneurial and see the need for a network that doesn't exist, you could start a new one. If it is field specific, advertise the network at a conference, if it is for a particular group at your workplace or in your profession, a workplace email or a link on a professional website might help connect you with those with similar needs. If there is interest in your network, ask your workplace and/or professional organization about office space and funding for catering or guest speakers.

Further reading

If you are looking for an affirming article that focuses on the ways that a non-hierarchical peer network can function to support career and identity development and its contribution to a sense of belonging, Martin, Mori, and Froehlich (2023) are a great read. Price, Coffey, and Nethery (2015) present an account of a network they developed. They discuss funding and detail things that worked and didn't work quite so well.

References

Martin, Annika; Mori, Julia, & Froehlich, Dominik Emanuel. (2023). Career development of early career researchers via distributed peer mentoring networks. *Merits, 3*, 569–582, https://doi.org/10.3390/merits3030034

Price, Emma; Coffey, Brian, & Nethery, Amy. (2015). An early career academic network: What worked and what didn't. *Journal of Further and Higher Education, 39*(5), 680–698, https://doi.org/10.1080/0309877X.2014.971106

10. Using administrative committee work to further your career

Administrative committees abound in every institution. Committee work adds to your workload, but proactive choices about which committee you join can help advance your career. Your initiative can both impress your boss and increase your ways of knowing and doing about your workplace. It puts you in a position to understand how and why decisions are made. This on-the-job professional development is valuable for understanding how you can best position you and your research within your organization (see Pointer 11).

Committee work also helps increase your visibility. It puts you in contact with senior staff, researchers, and some other great people. This means they know you. These connections can be a godsend if you need urgent or confidential help.

There are advantages to seeking out specific committee work. The most obvious one: you are less likely to be lumbered with committee work that doesn't suit you. When considering which administrative opportunities are best for you, reflect on how your ways of knowing, being, doing, and communicating fit the duties and responsibilities involved in the committee work. If your field of research is in health and safety, or student support, you could use your expertise to contribute in valuable ways. If you already have an in-depth knowledge of the content covered by the committee, the work will take less time out of your busy schedule.

Some types of committee work can contribute to your research productivity. For example, ethics committees give you valuable insight into how ethics applications should be worded and other important information that can make your future ethics application sail smoothly through approval. Ethics committee work also introduces you to a range of ways of doing research in ways that safeguard yourself and your research (see Pointer 6 for details on keeping yourself safe). Finally, when you have thorny ethical issues that you or your research candidates are fretting over, you have contacts that help you find solutions.

Volunteering for a research committee is another win-win situation. It increases your awareness of available grants for you and your doctoral candidates. You meet experienced researchers who can give feedback on your external grant application.

A library committee may open other opportunities. You may learn about new databases for literature searches and new programs to enable more comprehensive literature searches. Being part of a library committee gives you deeper knowledge of what resources the library has to offer, and who to contact for specific needs. Knowing library staff is like having friends who know all kinds of useful information, how to access it, and are willing to help.

Participating in committees outside your institution at the national or international levels has its advantages. It gives you far-reaching visibility as a researcher. You get to meet and interact with important researchers in your field, and you never know what advantages this might hold for you.

As in any career planning, it's important to research what your involvement entails. Find out how regularly the committee meets, in what format, and how much work might be undertaken between meetings (for example, are there lengthy documents to read and write before the meeting?). Ask before you sign up. It's also useful to limit your committee work, as any committee work takes time away from research. As in everything in life you need balance.

Once you gain experience on a committee, and you enjoy what you are doing, think about volunteering to act as the chair of the committee. It gives evidence of leadership that can enhance your CV and career success.

Further reading

Dodgen, Fowler, and Williams-Nickelson (2013) focus on the benefits of getting involved in professional organizations. They identify benefits that could equally apply elsewhere. Their comments on identity development gel well with many ideas we raise in pointers throughout this book.

Reference

Dodgen, Daniel; Fowler, Raymond D., & Williams-Nickelson, Carol. (2013). Getting involved in professional organizations: A gateway to career advancement. In Mitchell J. Prinstein & Marcus D. Patterson (Eds.), *The Portable Mentor: Expert Guide to a Successful Career in Psychology*, 257–267, Springer https://doi.org/10.1007/978-1-4614-3994-3

11. Finding yourself within institutional brands

Some ECRs revel in knowing and understanding the policies and practices of the institution where they work; others pay little attention to their existence. Whether you like it or not, some knowledge of policies around research can help you fast track your career.

Policies are driven by research institutions wanting to position themselves as leaders in specific fields (i.e., science education, architecture, etc.) or show how they contribute to big social issues (i.e., globalization, migration, climate change, etc.). Your organization wants (and often expects) you to help them with their endeavors, and this can be good for you. Aligning your research with the policy direction of your institution enables you to take advantage of what the institution has to offer. For example, if your workplace has a new policy that strongly encourages multidisciplinary research, they typically offer grants for those who take up the challenge.

There may be times when trying to conform can make you feel like you are losing part of your research identity, but it needn't be so. If you work in a university setting, the institutions won't want you to change your overall research plan or make changes overnight. Creative ECRs look for opportunities to make subtle and gradual changes to their research for maximum institutional impact. For example, if you conduct interviews and questionnaires as part of your ongoing research, you might add one or two questions to connect your research to the university brand. If policies promote research impact, you might try to develop community contacts or add an applied angle to your research. Mentors and academic support networks within your institution may be able to help if you need advice (see Pointers 8 and 9).

If change is hard for you, there are ways that you can often make educated guesses on your institution's future research directions for a head start. Research priorities are often influenced by how institutions are funded. Institutions receive funding (at least in part) through the government. Government priorities regarding research and education change every election (i.e., from multicultural issues to the importance of higher education, etc.). It helps to listen to what is on electoral agendas and its potential effects on you and your research. Sometimes you can get a heads-up within your organization. Upcoming changes are usually discussed there before the change is advertised throughout the organization. News items from management can also alert you to potential changes in institutional directions and how they might affect your research narrative (i.e., they may want you to add branding to your email correspondence, or alert you to changes in research leadership).

When your research and those of your institution are in alignment, it is often easier for you to promote your research through the media. When you appear on television, or in a radio interview, or on a podcast, the broadcasting agency promotes you, your work, and your institutional affiliation.[1]

Remember to add your achievement to your profile page and advertise it through other institutional channels (i.e., a departmental newsletter). A win for you is also a win for your institution.[2]

Finally, if you feel that you need to keep true to your research plan and focus on your long term goals, you could wait it out. Institutions rebrand every couple of years, or you could consider a career change to somewhere that is more appreciative of your kind of research. For some ECRs, this can be a much healthier alternative.

Further reading

Orazbayeva et al. (2019) analyze how universities, government, and businesses determine research priorities and how it feeds into ideas behind institutional branding.

Reference

Orazbayeva, Balzhan; Plewa, Carolin; Davey, Todd, & Muros, Victoria Galan. (2019). The future of university-business cooperation: Research and practice priorities. *Journal of Engineering and Technology Management, 54*, 67–80, DOI: 10.1016/j.jengtecman.2019.10.001

Notes

1. This includes helping develop awareness of what might be said in a public capacity. Before you appear publicly, contact the relevant body in your institution for approval and support. They typically have guidelines for those wanting a media profile as part of their research.
2. Remember, if you act in any official capacity, correspondence and promotional material should be through the institution's official email server or bear their logos, etc.

Your research
Publication

Overview

This chapter focuses on your publication agenda. The pointers put yourself front and center and ask you to think about your ways of being, doing, and communicating as you undertake your publication journey. The first pointer in this chapter delves into your publication plan and how to make your work have an impact. Further pointers offer strategic tips on getting published and hints on how to sell your ideas and maintain your voice. Final pointers concentrate on the highly emotional activity of receiving feedback and how you might use reviewers' comments to expand your publication ideas (Figure 5.1).

Figure 5.1 What's your publication plan?

12. What's your publication plan?

Knowing who you are as an ECR helps you choose what you want to research, how you wish to conduct your research, and how you communicate those ideas to the public. A vital part of disseminating your work is through publication. A publication plan aims to help you get started and stay focused. It gives you the clarity to confidently decline projects that do not align with what you want to do (now) and accept those that do.

Central to any publication plan is your brand. What idea do you want to be known for? This could be anything. If you are not entirely sure, start with your next potential publication and try working backward. What excites you about this potential work? Would you like your research career to continue in this direction? If so, great! If not, prepare yourself to move on to something different, perhaps after you finish your current work. Don't worry if the current work differs somewhat from your new narrative. Many researchers find themselves all over the place when they begin their careers.

The next step toward success is to make a list of what you want to achieve, short and long term. If pressed for time, you could focus on one or two items. You can always add more later.

If you want to explore ideas from your thesis, while the thesis is still fresh in your head, make these your first publications. As you think about your potential publications, explore the connection between what you plan to write and your future ECR identity. The ideas in your thesis may be a good reflection of your work in your imagined future, or your thesis ideas may be ones you want to finetune to align more with your future ECR identity and future work that you want to be known for.

If you already have work underway, all that might be required to bring together your work in progress with your new narrative is a sentence or two about the need for future work in specific areas. These sentences may be about ideas you wish to pursue or those you would like others to embark on.

If you are co-authoring any publications with your supervisor(s) on your thesis topic, have a frank conversation about where you would like to take your future career and your desire to embed this into ongoing work, if only in a small way. This discussion will make the writing journey much smoother. Your supervisors are likely to have useful ideas for rewording text to create an intended research niche when they know how you would like to craft your career.

To connect existing work to your future plans, footnotes also help. If you have a change of heart about how you have defined a key term, you can note your change of direction (or thinking) in a footnote in forthcoming publications. Starks and Robertson (2024), Pointer 29 provides details about good uses of footnotes.

At some point, your publication plan must look at ways of moving beyond your thesis. Loose ends from your thesis journey might provide you with a way forward, co-authors, mentors, and contacts within your academic networks are full of ideas if you need something to spur you on (see Chapter 6).

The second part of any successful publication plan involves projected timelines for publication. It's good to set tentative timelines, even if there are only one or two items in your first draft of your publication plan, or you are not quite sure when you might finish these works. Timelines don't need to be overly specific if this is not your thing. Your timelines might be as vague as a priority order, or perhaps time-focused, that is, within six months. Timelines for your publication plan work well when they include stages in the writing process (i.e., a first draft in six months) or steps in the writing process (i.e., you will present a conference paper on the topic at the next local conference). You could look at planning around both stages and processes in your publication plan (i.e., you will apply for funding to start the research before the end of the year).

Publication plans are not meant to be absolute. If it looks like you are not going to achieve a goal, it's okay to modify your plan. If something untoward occurs that affects your goals, it can be helpful to write a note next to your plan to remind you why life got in the way. This can help you think about changes to your ways of doing so you can adjust your ways for your next deadline or feel better about yourself if the thing that got in the way was something over which you had no control.

Finally, any publication plan needs to be realistic. If the list of potential publications in your publication plan is extensive, ask yourself how many publication projects you can take on now. It can be challenging to achieve quality finished products if you have too many competing deadlines.

Further reading

Chapter 34 in Allen and Golde (2018) provides a simple step-by-step guide for those writing a research article for the first time. If you are an ECR interested in turning your thesis into a book, Kubach et al. (2019) is a useful read, particularly Chapter 3 where the authors discuss the editorial process and the importance of producing a reader-friendly manuscript that fills a niche and sells it. Svantesson et al. (2019) have tidbits useful for all writers beginning their research journey.

References

Allen, Jan E., &Golde, Chris M. (2018). *The productive graduate student writer: How to manage your time, process, and energy to write your research proposal, thesis, and dissertation and get published*. Routledge.

Kubach, Douglas; Geiser, Elizabeth; Dolin, Arnold, & Topkis, Gladys. (2019). *The business of book publishing: Papers by practitioners*. Routledge.

Svantesson, Eleonor; Senorski, Eric Hamrin; Samuelsson, Kristian, & Karlsson, Jón. (2019, online). Common mistakes in manuscript writing and how to avoid them. In Musahl Volker et al. (Eds.), *Basic methods handbook for clinical orthopaedic research*, pp. 579–584. Springer. https://doi.org/10.1007/978-3-662-58254-1

If templates or planners help you think clearly, you may find the following links helpful:

https://www.bristol.ac.uk/media-library/sites/staffdevelopment/documents/rs-hub/research-publications-planner.pdf

https://www.editage.com/insights/how-to-create-a-publication-schedule-and-why

13. Making an impact through your publications

To have the most success in your career as a researcher, your intended publications need to make an impact. Impact can take many different forms. Your impact might be theoretical, methodological, or data driven. Your impact might be to question assumptions made by other researchers.

If you are now scratching your head about the impact of potential publications in your publication plan, start by focusing on the value of your ideas. They are there if you look!

The next step is to advertise this value in the introduction of your manuscript and reiterate that message at the end (see Pointer 16 on writing for selling your research). Making the value of your work explicit helps others understand and appreciate it.

When writing about your research impact, consider how your work could be of importance to others. You might explain why the type of research you are conducting is needed or how your research results can affect communities – socially, culturally, and/or economically. If the ideas and/or findings have potential implications for education, policy, politics, journalism, academia, business, science, or even the home, mention this.

Another way to make an impact is to guide others in their research. This is why many journals ask that the final section of your manuscript cover suggestions for future research. The ideas in these paragraphs have the potential to inspire researchers to pursue lines of research, change research directions, or extend their research in creative and interesting ways. In other words, research impact can be as simple as thinking about potential applications of your research and sharing those ideas. Researchers will cite you if you influence their research direction.

You could think about adding a manuscript to your publication plan with the sole purpose of evoking change. Would you like anything in your field to change for the betterment of your field or wider society? This could be a small change in assumptions about what is done, or how it is done, or what is yet to be done. Are there important issues you think should be raised but have not. Perhaps you could pose a potential solution to improve some aspect of your field (i.e., an innovation in methods could help improve others' research findings). Spreading new ideas is an important way of creating impact. You needn't take conventional approaches. Writing a short commentary in a blog or on a social network site can sometimes make more impact than publishing a journal article.

You can create impact and enact change outside academia. One way to achieve this is by sharing your expertise. This might be through an opinion piece in a local newspaper, a letter to the Editor, a blog, or a short piece for *The Conversation*, an interview on television or radio. If public speaking makes you feel uncomfortable, you might consider publishing a YouTube video, where you have time to plan and reflect on every aspect of what you communicate and how you communicate it. If making a YouTube video stretches your ECR ways of being and doing, seek support from experienced colleagues or mentors who have lived experiences with these genres. You might even consider co-authoring with them in your first video (see Pointer 7 for advice on choosing co-authors). If any of these ideas excite you, add them to your publication plan.

Think about working with those outside of academia. This can be a win-win. They introduce you to issues they need solved, and you can use your expertise to help them get their ideas out into the world (see Pointer 49 for other benefits).

If you are still at a loss for how you might use your research to enact change, try eliciting suggestions from others. If you teach in a university or school, perhaps you might end your undergraduate or graduate class with one or two potential ways of how you (or someone else) might apply knowledge learned in your class to a real-life context. If this becomes a routine way of concluding the class, you can give your students opportunities to share. With any luck, students will learn to think laterally and apply their ideas to their workplace, life, or research. Perhaps one of them might turn their idea into something truly important.

Finally, remember to monitor the impact of your publications through social media sites (see Pointer 3). There may be important information there that you can add to your CV.

Further reading

Aiello et al. (2021) consider different types of research impact, exemplify case studies of research that make a social impact and explore strategies you can use to achieve this. Denicolo (2014) introduces different types of research impact and discusses ways you can achieve this. She has a good discussion of how to describe your research impact in funding proposals.

References

Aiello, Emilia; Donovan, Clair; Duque, Elena, Fabrizio, Serena et al. (2021). Effective strategies that enhance the social impact of social sciences and humanities research. *Evidence & Policy*, *17*(1), 131–146, https://doi.org/10.1332/174426420X15834126054137

Denicolo, Pam (Ed.). (2013). *Achieving impact in research*. Sage.

14. Choosing publication formats for your publication plan

Books (monographs and edited volumes), book chapters, and journal articles (special issues and general submissions) have their ways of doing. Knowing the processes can help you understand which publication types work best for you, smooth your path forward, and avoid common pitfalls.

Books (monographs)

Books (monographs) are great if you have a piece of research that requires an extensive word count. Books can derive from a reworking of your thesis (see Pointer 48 in Starks & Robertson, 2024) or from work produced from a grant. Book publications work best when you have large amounts of data around a central issue.

If you have ample content for a book, the next step is to select the right book publisher. Your mentor or departmental or institutional research coordinator is the first point of call. They can often provide you with a short list of highly regarded publishing outlets in your research field.

Once you have a few potential outlets, it's time to read the fine print, even if this is something you dislike intensely. The fine print includes important details about the type of publication that the publisher is willing to accept. Some publishers are not keen on edited volumes with multiple authors, reworked theses, or academic works with a narrow market appeal. You don't want to be halfway through the book proposal before you realize you might need a different book publisher. Another important difference to look out for is what you need to submit as a book proposal. Some book publishers request a complete draft manuscript, others a sample chapter or two. If you need to produce an entire manuscript with your proposal, your proposal will take you much longer to compose, even if you are basing your book around their thesis.

The way you work is also important when considering which type of book proposal works best for you. If you are an ECR who changes your mind significantly during the writing process or you are unsure of the content of some potential chapters, it may be better to submit a book proposal with a complete draft of your manuscript. Alternatively, if you are an ECR with a carefully conceived and comprehensive plan about what to write, a book proposal that only asks for a few chapters can be faster to produce and provide you with a quicker outcome. An accepted book proposal gives you something special to add to your CV, promotion, or job application.

It's important to pay attention to the questions in a book proposal. These ask you to explain the aims of your book, its uses, and competing titles. The answers to these questions sell the merits of your proposed book to the publisher and show its market potential. If you haven't explained the aims of your book and considered the competition, your proposal may go nowhere. It's worthwhile taking time to craft your answers carefully.

Once you have submitted your proposal, the processes most publishers go through are similar. Your proposal will be sent to a nominated editor. If this editor sees the value of your manuscript, they will present their initial evaluation at a board meeting. These meetings usually happen once a month. The answers in the application form are key to your success. Manuscripts are often delayed (or rejected or asked to be reworked) if your answers don't fit the publisher's scope or requirements, or if the editor can't see a market (a readership) for your book. You don't want your proposal held up because you didn't give enough consideration to the marketing questions.

If the editorial board thinks your proposal has potential, it will be sent out for review. You cannot speed up these timelines, but you can craft your proposal for a potentially earlier response by writing in ways that sell your book (see Pointer 16 for ideas).

Some book editors take considerable time to get back to you. They may be having difficulty finding suitable reviewers, the reviewers may be slow getting back with their reviews, or both. If you have been waiting well over the recommended time frame provided by the book publisher, a brief email to your corresponding editor requesting an update on progress is appropriate.

Once your proposal is accepted, the publisher will draw up a contract. This is a legally binding document so read this very carefully. Check that the submission date is doable, and what obligations you may have (i.e., some publishers may require you to submit any further manuscripts that you write to them first). If you are happy with the contract, it is up to you to deliver. Timelines set by publishers are sometimes stricter than other forms of publication, so plan to complete your work ahead of schedule.[1] This can go against the grain of the ways of doing for some ECRs, but it is important. You need ample time to complete it. In addition to your manuscript, there is a surprising amount of additional stuff you need to send to the publishers (i.e., questionnaires, overviews of chapters for marketing, bios etc.) Plan for an early submission. Life events and writer's block can easily delay your writing.

Once you submit your completed manuscript to the publisher, your book is typically sent out for a final check to see if anything is missing or problematic (often to the same reviewers who thought your book was a great idea in the first place). At this stage, there are several potential outcomes. If you are lucky, you will receive approval to progress the manuscript to publication. The editorial team will read your book, respond with queries about sentences or paragraphs they can't follow or find clumsy, and then send the manuscript for proofreading. The editorial team will make minor edits and check your references, but having said that, they do appreciate a manuscript that reads well, has few typos, and correct references. At some later point, you will be given a set of galley proofs. Proofs have a quick turnaround time so plan your life to take a few days out of your routine to read them. If you know there is a period where you will not be able to read proofs (weddings, birthdays, conferences, etc.), let the editor know months in advance so they can look into making adjustments to their schedule to help with your needs.

Things don't always work out as planned. The publisher may decide that extra work is necessary before your manuscript can proceed. You may be asked to revise the content of a section in a chapter, or perhaps add a section or chapter. Or, you may be asked to take a completely different direction, one they think will better fit the market. In the latter case, the book editor may ask you to resubmit the proposal and accompanying manuscripts. If this occurs, you could buckle down and try their way, or you could try to submit your proposal elsewhere. If you approach another publisher, be prepared to rewrite your application and not cut and paste responses. Publishers often differ in the wording of the questions asked.

Book chapter or journal article in special issue

A second option in the publication game is to write smaller specialized works such as a book chapter or a journal article targeted to a special issue. These types of publications increase your potential readership. The other authors/editors of the volume will likely promote it in their prelude. Authors who publish in the volume receive a complimentary copy of your work. Because they publish on the same topic as you, they may read and cite your work. Readers who have an interest in a topic of the special issue or a specific article or chapter within it usually spend a few minutes skimming the entire volume. They may find your work of interest. If the editors of the edited book or special issue of the journal are well known, their followers will be notified about the volume and its table of contents. All of the above increases the chances of your work being cited.

Book chapters and journal articles in special issues have other advantages. They have less upfront work than general articles. Usually, all you have to write in the first instance is an abstract. If your abstract is spot on for the book or special issue topic and is well constructed with a novel idea, the abstract has a good chance of being accepted. Once the abstract is accepted, the editors generally work with you to help get your work published.

Yet, no type of publication is without its drawbacks. Opportunities to publish in a special issue or edited book on your research topic don't come up that often. Monitor regularly your professional and academic websites for opportunities so you don't miss out on potentially your one chance. It helps to be proactive in other ways. Not all opportunities are publicized on websites. Be on the lookout for special workshops on your topic at megaconferences, as these workshops often turn into edited volumes or special issues. Even if the workshop is closed to outside presenters or has more presenters than required, it can still be helpful to contact the workshop convenor. If the convenor knows about you and your work, they may review your publications and contact you if they have a gap in content in their volume. Someone might pull out. If nothing emerges from this correspondence, you can still write up your conference paper as a general submission to a journal knowing that if your topic relates to the subject of the megaconference workshop, it is timely, and editors like to publish on timely topics.

Another common downside with special issues and edited books is the time it takes to get to publication. Editors typically solicit abstracts from contributors before they submit a proposal for the book or special issue. This means they need to elicit and vet potential contributions and make decisions on abstracts they will accept. Once they have the abstracts they want, they need to ensure that all abstracts meet expectations and edit and revise any that need attention. Book editors and special series editors appreciate you completing any editing promptly, so you do not delay the whole project. Once all abstracts are finalized and the proposal is submitted to the journal or book publisher, there are two eventualities. If all goes well, things can progress. If the submitted proposal is rejected, another publisher needs to be found, and the wait time will be longer.

Once a publishing contract is secured, it can be smooth sailing if there are no tardy contributors, no contributors who have their submissions rejected, and no contributors who delay completing their revisions post-peer review. If this is the case, the editors need time with those authors or time to find other authors as replacements. This can add months to the process. If you are one of the authors who has been asked to rework a manuscript, do not delay. The editors are keen to get your manuscript to the press and will work with you to get there. They need your work to complete their volume.

If you are lucky and have few revisions, maintain regular (but not frequent) contact with the editor. You don't want to come across as a complainer!

A general submission to a journal

The most common form of publication is a general submission to a journal of your choosing. You decide on your topic and submit the manuscript when you feel it is ready.

The downside with this type of publication is that your entire manuscript must be submitted at the outset. This can be a problem if you submit a work that is not fully developed or crafted and your work is not accepted.

Where you publish is important. Institutional branding often pushes researchers to be visible on the international stage. Success can be difficult, and it can take years to get through the review process. You may want a mix of international and national publications to keep your publications coming out. The ultimate mix of publications will depend on your career direction. If you want a position in the best institutions, you will need to persist in trying to secure international publications with very good journal ratings.

Journal ratings are based on how frequently articles in the journal receive citations. If the journal has a rating, it will be located on the journal website. Alternatively, you will find lists of rankings in databases such as Scopus Sources or SCImago. If your workplace has a library, ask the librarian to help you access and download relevant journals in your field of expertise.

New journals may be an easy target to get started. They don't have a track history and are not rated. Many scholars won't submit their work to these journals and because of this, they can have fewer manuscript submissions. If you are not constrained by needing to publish in rated journals, you may want to submit your work here. You might get a request to revise and resubmit, rather than an outright rejection. In time, the journal is likely to become successful and get a rating, and it will be more difficult to get your work published. There are advantages to being first in.

When you submit your work as a general submission to a journal, there are a few processes involved. The editor will skim your work for journal fit, and if satisfied, they will request several reviewers for your manuscript. To secure reviewers, an editor typically sends out an email with a request to review your manuscript. The email typically contains two pieces of information: the manuscript title and abstract. Few editors send out the entire manuscript. While potential reviewers may decline to review a work if they don't think they have the requisite expertise, they often decline to review manuscripts for other reasons. If your title is unclear and your abstract is unpolished, it can give the impression that your article might be both time-consuming and difficult to review. If you want your manuscript to get through the review process, the better your abstract, the greater your chances of getting reviewers to agree to review your work (see Pointer 16 on selling your research).

If reviewers agree to read your manuscript and review it, they are requested to return their review within a set time and are prompted periodically to do so. Once the reports are in, if there is a significant difference in opinion between the reviewers (i.e., one says your work is great and a few minor edits are required, the other recommends it should be rejected), the editor may make a final decision or the editor may choose to send the manuscript out to additional reviewers. If that happens, you will be waiting a little longer.

If your manuscript is rejected, don't be too downhearted. You can choose another journal. Every scholar has at least one of their works rejected.

Further reading

If you are interested in the metrics of time around publication (how long is long enough and why this is happening), read Huismann and Smits (2017). Voight and Hoogenboom (2012) have presented this information in the form of a graphic. Both works can give you an understanding of what happens once you submit your manuscript for publication and where holdups in publication might occur.

References

Huisman, Janine, & Smits, Jeroen. (2017). Duration and quality of the peer review process: The author's perspective. *Scientometrics, 113*(1), 633–650, https://doi.org/10.1007/s11192-017-2310-5

Voight, Michael L., & Hoogenboom, Barbara J. (2012). Publishing your work in a journal: Understanding the peer review process. *International Journal of Sports Physical Therapy, 7*(5), 452–456.

15. Choose your journal then write your manuscript

Choosing a journal before you start to write your manuscript helps you design it for its potential home and avoid annoying last-minute changes. If you know the required word limits of your manuscript, you can write to these limits, and you won't have to reduce your work from 8,000 words to 5,000 words because it is over the word limit.

When you know where you want to publish, you can plan your writing to fit journal requirements. Every journal prefers its articles to be written in a particular way. If your introduction to your desired journal needs to include/exclude a detailed literature review, when you begin to compose your text, you can write your text in ways that make it conform. If the journal requires specific types of information in the conclusion (i.e., implications of your research, or future directions for research in this area), you can plan to include this information in your writing. If you don't know where you want to publish until after you complete your manuscript, you will find it difficult to include any extra requirements if you are close to the journal's word limits. If you target a journal, you also know which formatting conventions to use and you won't have to deal with formatting changes later. This can save days if not weeks of editing.

Designing your publication to fit your intended publication outlet has other advantages; ones that increase your chances of getting published. If you know your intended publication outlet, you can write with the aims of the outlet in mind. You can compose your introduction to bring to the fore how your work fits with the aims of the journal and word your research questions in ways that are pertinent to the publication outlet. You can also structure your literature review by drawing on works and arguments from the journal.

There are other advantages to working your research up for a specific publication outlet. Editors prefer referees they have worked with before. If there are authors who have previously published on the same topic in your desired publication outlet, they may be asked to review your work. This can work to your advantage. If you have crafted your text to fit this journal outlet, you are already aware of the arguments these potential referees deem important. This knowledge can help you craft your manuscript in ways that will tempt those referees to review your manuscript.

If you are unsure which journals to choose, there are a few factors to consider. Some publication outlets come with great prestige and can help further your career. Others have no prestige (i.e., everything is accepted with no peer review process). In the latter journals, you get little benefit from publishing in them.

If your supervisor or mentor publishes in an area close to your topic, check their list of publications in their CV for ideas. Then ask your supervisor or mentor for their advice so you target the right sort of publication outlets. They will be able to tell you about their experiences with these publishers.

Publishers vary greatly in the time they take to work through your manuscript before they reach a decision. Some have efficient editorial processes; others are not so efficient. Different disciplines and fields also vary greatly in response times. Your colleagues and mentors have lived experiences with a wide variety of publication outlets and know of those that might give you a quick turnaround. This can be especially important if you need publications urgently (i.e., you are up for promotion, your contract is up for renewal, you need this publication for a grant or job application, etc.).

It is equally important that you do not submit your manuscript and forget about it. With each manuscript you submit, you should receive an acknowledgement from the publisher that your manuscript has been received. This usually happens within a couple of days of your submission, and increasingly that acknowledgement is listed on the submission website. If you don't receive any notification (or see it on the submission website) within a few weeks, it helps to check with the editor. You wouldn't be the first author to have experienced a glitch in a submission system. In rare cases, you might have to relodge your work in their system. A good editor will work extra hard to get your manuscript reviewed to make up for the earlier delay on their part.

One place where your publication may stall is with the review process. A response can take three to eight months (sometimes longer). The timing depends on many factors (i.e., finding suitable reviewers, editor workloads, etc.). It can also depend on the nature of your publication (see Pointer 15 on book chapters). Keep your submission date handy and if the publisher doesn't adhere to their stated guidelines for returning work with feedback, one month after your nominated date, send them an email to ask about the status of your manuscript.

It is also good to model yourself after highly productive ECRs. They always start another publication while they wait.

Further reading

Knight and Steinbach (2008) provide a comprehensive discussion of things to consider when selecting among suitable journal outlets. Their work covers a range of disciplines and explains the logic behind why some journals have better reputations than others. This work contains visual displays of information that can assist those who appreciate information presented in this way. While not the focus of their publication, the principles in Knight and Steinbach's work are useful when selecting book publishers.

Reference

Knight, Linda V., & Steinbach, Theresa A. (2008). Selecting an appropriate publication outlet: A comprehensive model of journal selection criteria for researchers in a broad range of academic disciplines. *International Journal of Doctoral Studies, 3*, 59–79.

16. Hints for writing: getting published

Your publication plan is only as good as its outcomes. This means you need to get your work published. You need to convince your audience (editors, reviewers, readers) that the content of your manuscript makes not simply a point, but an important one. This means you need to write your work in a way that sells your idea.

Selling your research starts with your title. The importance of your title cannot be overstated. Your title needs to catch the interest of the journal editor. With hundreds of articles to shift through, your work must stand out to get on the top of the manuscript pile. If it doesn't have a clear title, the editor needs to expend more energy to look for its merit. A clear, informative purposeful title gives you a head start. A vague title leaves the editor guessing or worse, it leads them in the wrong direction.

Your abstract is the next critical step as it sells your manuscript as an appropriate work for the journal. It needs to contain enough content for the editor to judge whether the manuscript fits the journal remit. It helps to look at the topics covered in the journal and include one of those keywords in your abstract.

Once the abstract is deemed to fit the journal, you need to sell the value of your research. Your abstract must show that your work challenges an existing idea, or it builds on existing ideas in interesting and useful ways (see Pointer 13 on impact). You might check your verbs in your abstract. Can you strengthen them? A verb such as 'describe' creates a different impression about the value of your research than a verb such as 'argue' or 'demonstrate'.

Your abstract also helps to entice the editor and reviewers to read your manuscript. It must be lucid and grammatically correct. Judging the readability of your text can be difficult. Your sentences might be dense if you have been trying to meet the word limits. You may have too many points in a single sentence. You may have covered more detail than you need. Getting feedback on your abstract before submitting is invaluable. If anyone suggests a sentence in your abstract is confusing or needs reading twice before it is clear, don't question the feedback – rewrite the sentence.

Finally, your abstract needs to align perfectly with the content of your paper. An editor reads your abstract first, and this sticks in their head, and they judge the rest of your manuscript from this content.

Check your manuscript against what you have written in the rest of your manuscript. It is easy for your ideas in your abstract to no longer reflect all ideas in your manuscript. You may have promised more than you delivered. Check also that the key terms in your abstract are ones that are used in the rest of your manuscript. If you use a word to describe a key term in your abstract, you must ensure that you use that term throughout your manuscript.

With so much to think about when writing an abstract, writers' manuals often suggest that you write your abstract at the end of your writing journey. Whenever you choose to write the abstract, remember that a good abstract is worth the time it takes to perfect it. Writing abstracts is a foundational skill, not only for journal articles but for many academic purposes: selling courses, attracting graduate students (Pointer 31), writing successful grant proposals (Pointer 26), etc.

The next selling point in your manuscript is in its introductory section. The selling of your introduction is twofold. First, as noted earlier, the content must align with the abstract. Second, the introduction must explain clearly what the manuscript is about so the editor and reviewers can judge why it is important. A gap in the literature is only important if you show why the gap needs to be filled. If you have not articulated what is special about your research topic and its worth in your introductory paragraphs, the manuscript may not get a positive review. Most reviewers will form an opinion about the worth of your paper based on your introduction. If they think the introductory section of your manuscript has merit, they often read the rest of your manuscript with an eye to ways of improving your work. If they see little merit in your introduction, they often read your manuscript with its shortcomings in mind.

Finally, when you write your introduction, you could consider personalizing it a little. You might briefly mention why the topic or issue is important to you. A personal perspective helps reviewers develop rapport with you. A reviewer who can see you in your work is often kinder in their reviews.

Once your introduction is written, you are ready to let your reviewers read the rest of your paper.

Further reading

Dewan and Gupta (2016) outline the principles of writing titles, abstracts, and introductions. Although their examples come from medical fields, their advice applies to all disciplines. Their article offers good advice on organizing paragraphs and using summary statements. Tullu (2019) focuses on creating titles and abstracts that get work published and cited.

References

Dewan, Pooja, & Gupta, Piyush. (2016). Writing the title, abstract and introduction: Looks matter! *Indian Pediatrics, 53*, 235–241.
Tullu, Milind. S. (2019). Writing the title and abstract for a research paper: Being concise, precise, and meticulous is the key. *Saudi Journal of Anaesthesia, 13*(1), S12–S17, DOI: 10.4103/sja.SJA_685_18

17. Receiving feedback

You have been working on a manuscript and feel it is almost ready for the publishers. You are emotionally drained from all your hard work, and you have other pressing things that need immediate attention. No matter what your situation, it is wise to elicit feedback from a critical reader before you submit your work.

To get feedback to work for you, you need to let your critical friend know when you need their help so they can timetable it into your schedule and report back to you on time. Everyone has a busy schedule.

You also need to let them know what type of feedback you want. Setting your parameters before you ask for their help makes everything flow more smoothly. The more extensive the feedback you require, the longer your critical friends will need. If you only have time for your critical friend to give you a quick scan to assure yourself that your manuscript is ready to submit, ensure that you tell your critical friend this. With this in mind, a critical friend can give your manuscript a quick glance and suggest small final touches to help get it accepted. A quick proofread will pick up typos, find a sentence or two needing a reformulation, query a point that requires a sentence more to clarify, or note missing bibliographical references. All are easy fixes that give you confidence in your work and energize you to keep your career moving forward.

If you have a little more time, energy, and confidence, you could ask a critical friend for more detailed feedback. You might ask them to pay attention to those parts of your manuscript that are causing you concern. For example, you could ask for feedback on your abstract. If the abstract or introduction isn't convincing, your manuscript will not get past an editor's desk review (see Pointer 16 for details). You could ask them to tease through your methodology section to check that all necessary information is there and presented in the right order. A convincing methodology solidifies your manuscript.

If you have embedded into your publication plan more time for feedback, you could elicit feedback from more than one critical friend. The more feedback you get, the fewer things your reviewers need to criticize, and the quicker they can respond.

When you ask more than one critical friend to review your work, sequencing the feedback is important. Sending out your manuscript to all critical friends simultaneously may seem faster but collating comments takes time and is frustrating when there is more than a little to change. It is also kinder to your critical friends as it saves them all from repeating the same comments. When asking for sequenced feedback, consider what each critical friend can offer your manuscript. A critical friend who sees the bigger picture is better to review your work first, as their constructive critique may involve reworking ideas and text.

Finally, while feedback enhances the content and wording of your manuscript, remember to check what they have suggested. Look carefully at the terminology that critical friends may have offered and whether it differs from yours. You don't want to introduce new terms unnecessarily into your text. If any feedback includes a brilliant sentence or key term (written by an experienced reviewer who writes in ways you like), you could try to adopt that wording throughout your text and in other future work. Ways of communicating can always be improved.

Finally, if you receive feedback, you should be willing to give it. Before you offer to be a critical friend, decide which types of feedback you are particularly good at (i.e., topic sentences, flow, typos, etc.) and offer to provide that feedback. You might also offer to review a manuscript or two for a journal. When you give feedback, think about how long it takes you to complete it. Look at your tone to see how polite you were. You don't want to alienate your friends or dissuade someone from revising and resubmitting their manuscript by being too abrupt in your commentary. Similarly, saying all good things is great for morale, but it doesn't help improve the manuscript. You need a balance. If you have received comments from reviewers asking you to revise your work, think about how these comments made you feel.

Further reading

Caffarella and Barnett (2000) discuss the benefits of receiving and giving critical feedback for writer development. This article acknowledges that receiving feedback can be frustrating and highly emotional. Mathioudakis et al. (2022) offer insights into providing others with feedback. Their work gives advice when editing writing.

References

Caffarella, Rosemary S., &Barnett, Bruce G. (2000). Teaching doctoral students to become scholarly writers: The importance of giving and receiving critiques. *Studies in Higher Education, 25*(1), 39–52.

Mathioudakis, Alexander G.; Wagner, Darcy, & Bumas, Orianne. (2022). How to peer review: Practical advice for early career researchers. *Breathe, 18*(4), 1–10, https://doi.org/10.1183/20734735.0160-2022

18. Your voice in publications

Before you finalize your manuscript and submit it for publication, reflect on your ways of communicating and whether you could do anything more to make your voice stand out. There are particular things that can distance your voice from your text. Quotes can cause chaos in your text. While the content of the message in a quote often melds with your ways of thinking and if the theoretical positioning is the same as your ways of knowing, it can meld with your ways of knowing. However, your ways of communicating are usually not in sync. It is hard to fit your voice with their words.

You and the author of the quote have different writing styles. The author of the quote might have used a passive sentence, written in the past tense, and/or used the third person. Your surrounding text might be written in an active voice, or be written in the present tense, and perhaps you in the first person. In the surrounding text, you might have used 'can' as a modal verb to reflect possibility, the quote might have used 'may'. There might even be differences in spelling (i.e., British vs American). Unless you are using the quote as an example of something you disagree with (where subtle differences in style can help to construct an implicit argument against what is written in the quote), the disjuncture can affect the flow of your text.

There are ways to get around some of the disjuncture. You can help reconcile the original quote with your intended focus by eclipsing parts of the quote with '[…]' to bring only the part of the content that you want to highlight to the fore.

Another way of avoiding disjuncture and bringing the text together is to bridge the transition between the quote and your text by adding a sentence in your surrounding text about how what is written in the quote supports the point you are trying to make. Such a statement makes the content of the quote more salient to your reader and helps instill your voice as the only dominant one. If this sentence is challenging to construct, consider whether the words or intent behind the quote enhance your argument. You might consider whether you need the quote at all. Often, you are better off paraphrasing their ideas into your own words.

The second place when voices may conflict is in co-authored works. Each author has a unique voice, and it can be challenging for the text to come across as coherent if different authors write different sections. To achieve greater coherence in the text, having one person from your team undertake the final edit of the draft manuscript will give the text a more consistent voice. However, check first whether the co-author who isn't involved in editing the final draft feels that they have lost some ownership over their work by not participating in the final edit. Another approach is to co-construct part of the manuscript to develop a united voice. Once you have compiled a full manuscript draft, take turns editing the draft manuscript until your voices meld into one. For this to work, you need to discuss why changes are being made. If one author likes an impersonal style and another a more personal style, a consensus (or at least a compromise) will be needed for the text to flow. While getting a united voice can take lots of time, energy, and a lot of patience, the process gets easier over time and everyone will emerge a better writer. If there is no consensus, you could get an independent proofreader to highlight bits of the text that stand out to them as originating from different voices. You can focus your editing on these bits.

A third place where the voice of others can creep into your manuscript is when you receive feedback from critical friends (see Pointer 16), and when you deal with reviewer comments (see Pointer 19).

Further reading

Starks and Robertson (2024) contain detailed information about writing your voice into your thesis. While the text is written for thesis candidates, the recommendations in this book are applicable to writing journal articles, book chapters, or even an entire book.

Reference

Starks, Donna, & Robertson, Margaret J. (2024). *Fifty things to think about when writing your thesis: Paving your way to submission*. Routledge.

19. Turning reviewer comments into new writing ideas

Everything has so far gone to plan. You had a research idea, conducted the research, and submitted the manuscript for publication. After months of anticipation, you have received an email response from the journal, asking you to rework at least some parts of the manuscript. While many ECRs want to get the changes over with, it can be useful to read this email carefully. Comments in the feedback often contain seeds of inspiration for improving your manuscript and sometimes creating a second one. This pointer focuses on the latter possibility.

Reviewer comments might ask you to delete a part of your manuscript because they think that point doesn't fit well in your manuscript. It is relatively common for researchers with many ideas to put more of them in a manuscript than required. Instead of stressing about removing parts of your text, consider the value of what you are deleting. Could it be something you could add as an idea to your publication plan?

The content you have been asked to remove might be only a short paragraph or two. However, the topic of the original manuscript and the content of this paragraph share bits in common, some of the basic ideas will be the same. You may use the same theoretical underpinnings and methodology. You only need to rework the text into another story – one that perhaps draws on different key points in your theory and highlights other parts of your methods. To help avoid inadvertently self-plagiarizing, it's important to rewrite your original text rather than cut and paste bits out of the original. It's easy to do when you have ideas to put into words.

Another possibility for a new manuscript is when the reviewers ask you to consider a different perspective. Perhaps they may want you to consider a different theoretical theory, a different means of collecting your data, or they want you to ask another research question. When they provide this kind of critique you may think this too hard and want to try your luck with another journal. This may be the best option for you. However, before you discard the feedback, consider carefully the comments from the reviewers. Are any of the ideas interesting to you? Might any provide you with another direction and potentially another publication that you might add to your publication plan? If the suggestions involve lots of work in an area that you know little about, is there a co-author you could add to help you achieve this different direction (see Pointer 7 on co-authoring)?

Further reading

While a little dated, Chapter 26 in Osipow (2006) holds valuable advice on reviewer feedback.

Reference

Osipow, Samuel. (2006). Dealing with journal editors and reviews. In Fredrick T.L. Leong & James T. Austin (Eds.), *The psychology research handbook: A guide for graduate students and research assistant,* pp. 381–386. (2nd ed.) Sage. https://doi.org/10.4135/9781412976626

Note

1 If your circumstances change and it is impossible to meet the submission date, contact your publisher as soon as you realize to explain your circumstances. They may agree to modify the contract. If your writing has gone surprisingly well, you can contact the publisher to discuss moving the submission date forward.

Progressing your research with (or without) funding

Overview

This chapter emphasizes the importance of putting you at the center of all your funding applications. This chapter considers how you might build a strong and coherent narrative to help your grant success. This chapter starts with pointers that explore early grant preparation to enhance your research strengths. These pointers cover working as part of someone else's team, working on research projects without large scale funding, and building community links. Later pointers move to ways of securing funds. These pointers explore how to evaluate funding sources, what to look for when reading application forms, and alternative funding sources. The pointers then turn to ways of enhancing your application. These include selling your ideas and promoting what is special about you and your team. The final pointers focus on preparing a budget and grant management (Figure 6.1).

Figure 6.1 Small successes lead to bigger grants.

DOI: 10.4324/9781003481034-6

20. Working as part of someone else's team

Joining someone else's grant-funded team can help you gain confidence in your abilities, learn new ways of doing that build your CV and help you write your own funding application.

To ensure a position works for you, ask questions that drill down into the research project and your role in it to explore what the position offers you. It also helps to prepare a range of pitches. This needs to include statements about your strengths and your desires for opportunities to learn new ways of doing. These pitches open opportunities for you to take on tasks that you might not get otherwise. If you are shy, you may need to practice pitches with friends beforehand.

It also helps to ask about any perks of the position before you start your position. This might include research funding, co-supervision, publications (and in rare instances, first authorship), etc. It's hard to change the terms of your contract after the fact. See Pointer 47 for further information on preparing for interviews.

If you started on a grant-funded research project before you completed your doctoral research, and you are still working on this project, request a meeting with the lead researcher(s). As an ECR, explain that you are a different person than when you were a doctoral researcher. You have a new identity and new thoughts about how you would like to be positioned in the team to help fill gaps in your CV.

For both new and existing teams, it helps to let the team know about your ultimate plans to write your own major funding application as a lead researcher. When researchers know your long term game plan, they are often more willing to give you more responsibilities and answer questions explaining why research is completed in certain ways. This will help you understand the bigger picture of how grants work. If the lead researchers are applying for new funding, ask if you can sit in on any meetings, and read and respond to draft proposals. There is much to learn from how established researchers frame their ideas.

If the project has a grant manager, talk to them about the day-to-day running, what is involved and pitfalls to avoid. Titbits from these discussions can save your budget. Ask the other team members how their roles contribute to the project. These kinds of details will help you compose your grant application. You might even find a potential future co-researcher through these discussions.

It's also important to give information freely. If you have ideas about how things in the current project might be run differently, speak up. Your team may appreciate your suggestions and run with them. Alternatively, if they don't like the idea, they may point out why this won't work, saving you from making a poor suggestion in your future grant application. Keep careful track of any learning. It's easy to forget small but important points when the time comes to write parts of your funding application.

Finally, be mindful of your timelines so that you can complete your funding application before the end of your contract. Write small parts of your proposal on an ongoing basis. If you are super busy, set small achievable targets that you can meet. It may only be a paragraph a week. See Pointer 12 for further ideas.

If you feel that you are not learning much from your position, or if the position is time-consuming, leaving you exhausted and unable to craft your funding application when you get home from work, it might be time to look for other opportunities. See Pointer 49 for suggestions for when your position doesn't go as expected and what you might do about it.

Further reading

O'Cathain, Murphy, and Nicholl (2008) interviewed researchers who worked in multidisciplinary teams. The authors cover many facets of team research, including common pitfalls. Siltanen, Willibi, and Scobie (2008) expose the collaborative nature of team research. This is a useful paper for those interested in searching for ways of combining alternative ways of being and doing in their research.

References

O'Cathain, Alicia; Murphy, Elizabeth, & Nicholl, Jon. (2008). Multidisciplinary, interdisciplinary, or dysfunctional? Team working in mixed-methods research. *Qualitative Health Research*, *18*(11), 1574–1585.

Siltanen, Janet; Willibi, Alette, & Scobie, Willow. (2008). Separately together: Working reflexively as a team. *International Journal of Social Research*, *11*(1), 45–61. https://doi.org/10.1080/13645570701622116

21. Starting on your own with unfunded research

Do you have a research idea that you would like to turn into a project? If you are an ECR still searching for employment or have a full time position that doesn't involve research, you can embark on your research journey with little or no funding.

If you are commencing research without funding, some strategies might help. Scaling down your research goals to explore one part of a research idea is a strategic way to start. It can give you a clearer idea of your needs, including how long your project might take, and open ideas about how everything needs to fit together. It can also give you the confidence to continue.

Doing a small part of your research on your own also puts you in a stronger position to sort out what help might be the most useful and what questions you need to answer to scale up your project.

One useful place to start is to search through recent literature to ensure that your research idea is novel. Look closely at any suggestions in articles about future research. You don't want to go too far into your research without knowing for certain that you are filling a needed niche.

Depending on how you prefer to work, as you read the literature, you might compile written instructions to help future research team members stay focused when your future team completes a more extensive literature review. You might compile a set of comprehensive questions to ask each article (i.e., does the article answer the following questions (partly or fully), and if so how), and/or create formal templates to help organize and keep track of any reading.

There are other options to get you started. If you have ideas about two or three key research questions but are uncertain if the proposed wording will elicit optimal responses, you could crowdsource how well the questions might work through a short online survey. See also Pointer 3 on using social media for your research. Online surveys have benefits. Many are free, others can be available free of cost through an employer or library.[1]

Ethics applications are either unnecessary or minimal when online responses are elicited anonymously from the public. Online surveys do some of the analysis for you. The data does not need to be transcribed, and most electronic surveys come with tools that provide multiple options for compiling and sorting data to look at survey results from different angles. To get the most out of online surveys, keep your questions to a minimum and carefully consider whether any background questions are needed for the purposes at hand. There is an inverse relationship between the number of questions asked and the number of willing participants.

Suppose your intended funding application involves community research. In that case, another potential way to start planning for your funding application is to complete a short interview with a community gatekeeper (e.g., a principal at a school, a mayor, an elder, etc.) about the suitability of your research and the appropriacy of your wording of key research questions. Conducting an open-ended interview with a community gatekeeper allows you to explain your project and listen to feedback. Consider asking open-ended questions that elicit information about their views on your intended research. Do they see your work as valuable for their community? Could your project be of more value if part of the project was focused on another direction? Is there a way of framing the project that might work better? A community gatekeeper can provide insider information about what might work and what mightn't. Your interview can also have a useful spin-off effect. An interested and informed gatekeeper will spread news about your project and encourage community members to become involved. For further insights on community involvement, see Pointer 22.

While these small steps might not give you enough data for a strong publication in a top journal, they may provide enough findings to get your idea out in the public sphere. A short literature review and an interview with the gatekeeper; or a few results from an online survey about the benefits of checking the wording of research questions could provide you with enough information to compose a commentary or a short note in a local journal or newspaper or help you to write a blog entry. Once you have something in print, this opens further opportunities for you to write a piece for *The Conversation* and establish further ownership over your idea. This can be important if you are an ECR working on a time sensitive project. Any such publications also build your CV, a vital ingredient for grant success. You might even present your preliminary findings at a conference. See Pointer 4 on conferences for further insights.

Any small steps you achieve show initiative and commitment and are seen positively when funding agencies read your future application.

Further reading

Goldsworthy (2008) is a useful read for those considering applying for funding primarily because they think they should do so. Hay's (2017) chapter on 'Managing your time' is a great resource for meeting deadlines. We recommend that you download Hay's entire book. It has chapters on grant writing, and advice on writing CVs, teaching, research, and mentoring.

References

Goldsworthy, Jeffrey. (2008). Research grant mania. *The Australian Universities Review, 50*(2), 17–24.

Hay, Iain. (2017). Manage your time. In *How to be an academic superhero: Establishing and sustaining a successful career in the social sciences and arts and humanities.* Edward Elgar. https://doi.org/10.4337/9781786438126.00025

22. Working with community-based research

If you are interested in community-based research, the sooner you let your intentions be known, the better. This means contacting the community before you apply for any funding. It's the polite thing to do and there are many rewards to reap by letting the community know about your plans before you secure any major funding. Discussing your ideas with your proposed research community at the outset of your project helps gain community interest and support, deal with questions and apprehensions, and evoke change for greater community impact (see Pointer 21 on starting without research funding). The earlier you begin discussions; the more time you will have to build critical relationships to make your project work for you and the community.

Any community-based research projects need to be seen as mutually beneficial. This means looking for ways of giving back to the community. If you intend to work on a community research project, could community members work on your project as research assistants? Could community members be engaged as core members of your research team? Perhaps you could mentor someone from the community to be a researcher of the future? Including the community in these ways involves budgeting considerations, so it is best done before you begin applying for any funding.

There are other ways to give back to the community. As an academic, you have useful lived experiences and ways of knowing, doing, and communicating. You could offer to review community funding applications or write a letter to the government on an important community issue. You may know how to set up a crowdfunding site, or a blog for the community. Perhaps you could advise how high school students might think about university assignments, pitfalls to look out for and where they might find mentorship and support. This kind of leadership has long term effects and can open doors for you and other researchers who want to conduct research in the future.

You could give back to the community by participating in their activities. You might contribute to regular community events. You could volunteer to help set up an event, deliver goods, staff a booth or desk, or help clean up. Before you offer, think about your time commitments. You don't want to overcommit and renege on any offer.

If you are leading a research team, consider what the whole team can contribute. The more members of your team who contribute to the community, the more likely the community is to associate the work with the project (and not just you).

Finally, don't overlook the importance of maintaining contact after you have collected your data. Take regular opportunities to reconnect. If you are relatively close, continue to attend community events or send a team member on your behalf. If you can't physically travel to the research community, find a way to organize small tokens of your appreciation. You might arrange for a cake to be dropped off at a special community morning tea or support the school team if they happen to be playing near you. You might continue to offer your services and specialized skills when you can. It's important to retain contact with the community and not let them feel that they have been abandoned once the data collection is complete.

Further reading

Koster, Baccar, and Lemelin (2012) describe a research project with Indigenous communities in Canada and how the researchers worked within communities to achieve mutual goals. Other researchers look into why they started their research projects. For example, McCallum (2017) explores the social reasons many African Americans have for starting a PhD. Many ECRs embark on research in their communities where they bring in-depth knowledge of the community and their needs.

References

Koster, Rhonda; Baccar, Kirstine, & Lemelin, R. Harvey. (2012). Moving from research ON, to research WITH and FOR Indigenous communities: A critical reflection on community-based participatory research. *Canadian Geographer, 12,* 195–210. https://doi.org/10.1111/j.1541-0064.2012.00428.x

McCallum, Carmen. (2017). Giving back to the community: How African Americans envision utilizing their PhD. *The Journal of Negro Education, 86*(2), 138–53. https://doi.org/10.7709/jnegroeducation.86.2.0138

23. Exploring all possible funding

There is only so much research that you can do without funding. Funds are a necessary part of most research. Some research positions come with substantial funding attached; others come with limited funds; and some have none. This could be an important selling point if you are fortunate enough to have more than one job offer.

Sometimes, funding is 'in kind'. Some positions have research support to help researchers complete basic research tasks (i.e., a pool of available research assistants). These funds might only be available if you raise the issue of research funding when you interview for your position (see Pointer 47 on interviews).

Another source of easy in-house funds can become available at the end of each financial year. It's important to keep your eyes out for any email from your place of work offering small pots of funds to those who can see opportunities for the money to be spent immediately. These funds are often open to everyone on staff and require little in the form of an application. If you can't use these funds when they are available, don't bother applying. There will be future opportunities.

If you hold a full-time position, numerous internal research funds might be available to you. There may be grants at every level of your employment: from institutional grants to grants run through research centers, schools, and departments. All offer opportunities. The big question is: which grants are the best ones for you right here and now? Different grants fund different sorts of things and suit different stages of research. Ask those who have worked in your institution for a while if they can suggest which grant might have the best chance of success. If you don't ask, you won't know.

Check if there are time limits on internal funds. Grants for new staff need to be accessed within the first months or year(s) of employment. Other grants are tailored more broadly to ECRs but must be accessed within a few years of attaining your degree. You don't want to waste these opportunities. Not every ECR has ready access to internal funding. If you are employed in sessional or casual work, you may not be eligible to apply as the lead researcher. You might want to explore the possibility of working as a co-researcher with a senior researcher (i.e., your mentor, or a colleague) who might consider putting in an application with you. This option is not for every ECR. You must be willing to concede 'official' leadership on the grant to get your projects moving. This requires careful dialogue to ensure you get what you want from the arrangement (i.e., first authorship on at least some publications).

If you have exhausted all possibilities for internal funding possibilities within your institution (or don't have access to any such funding), there are opportunities elsewhere. Professional associations have small pots of funds for their members. Before paying for membership, check out what is on offer and whether the professional association offers discounted membership fees to those not in full-time employment.

You can search further afield for small (and sometimes large) pots of research funds. Community groups, government bodies, philanthropic organizations, and even private citizens fund research. Any research office will have an extensive list of external granting agencies.

Searching for grants can be exhausting. Consider all pertinent information about you before you search out external grants. You may be eligible to apply for a grant just because of who you are. There are grants specific for women, LGBTIQ+, those with disabilities, older people, and people of specific ethnic backgrounds or nationalities. There are even grants for those with family connections such as those who are children of military servicemen and those whose families belong to groups such as Rotary or Masons. Ask family members if they belong to organizations and check online if these organizations fund research. Grants with restricted eligibility often have fewer applicants and a greater chance of success.

Further reading

Khoo, Ward, and O'Donnell's introductory chapter, 'Learn how to ask for money' is a first point of call. This resource provides an excellent introduction to various available grants and helpful pointers for constructing a grant application. There is useful information about grant writing on websites such as: https://www.thegrantshub.com.au/blog/articles/top-10-tips-for-successful-grant-writing.

Reference

Khoo, Tseen; Ward, Phil, & O'Donnell, Jonathan. (2023). *Getting research funded: Five essential rules for Early Career Researchers*. Routledge.

24. Assessing grants for the right fit

Once you have located a few potential grants that might help fund your research, you need to decide among them. Grant applications come in different shapes and sizes. Some grant applications are short and straightforward, others are lengthy and detailed requiring extensive text about what you plan to do and why. While shorter applications may be the most tempting, it's important not to discard longer applications because they take up more of your time. Writing detailed descriptions of your planned project can be time well spent. Long applications are useful for expanding and finetuning your ideas.

Sometimes it isn't the length of the application but one or two of the questions in the application that strike fear in your heart. Grant applications can contain questions that are challenging to answer (i.e., questions about community benefits if this isn't the focus of your research). Before discarding any potential application, seek out mentors with experience in grant writing for potential ideas. You might be pleasantly surprised by what your mentors suggest. A couple of well-chosen words (i.e., the grant employs methods that could be used to investigate real-life problems in fields such as….) may be all that you need to answer a question convincingly.

There may be some application questions that leave you without answers. Instead of giving up, consider whether you might tweak your project to make your research fit. An extra survey or interview question might be all you need.

Budgets are another area that differs among potential funding sources. Grants fund small research projects from under $500 up to multimillion-dollar projects. If there is a grant that you are eligible to apply for and you only need a tenth of the amount on offer, it is better to wait for your research to develop before you apply. Conversely, before discarding an application for small funds that do not meet your financial needs, consider any non-financial benefits the grant may offer. A small successful grant can be used to fill a gap in your research profile. It may be used to show that you are dedicated to a particular issue (i.e., diversity and inclusion) or perhaps offer support for your research community. A series of small grants are often easier to apply for and succeed in obtaining than one larger one. Together a collection of small grants establishes a successful funding profile and increases your chances of later success with a larger grant.

The second budget issue in a grant application concerns expenses covered. While some grants allow you relative freedom, others do not. Some fund large equipment purchases, but not small equipment purchases. Some don't fund research assistants and researchers. Some exclude gifts to participants or catering for participant recruitment events. Read the fine print carefully before applying. If an application covers some of your needs, consider whether you can split your requests for funding across multiple grant applications. If this appeals to you, pay particular attention to whether the funding sources fund new projects. A project that builds on previous research might be conceptualized and presented as new if it is distinct in some way from prior research. Is it possible for your research to be separated and presented as two different studies? One application might cover theoretical aspects of your work, the other might apply that blue sky research. One application might fund research that answers your first research question while another might fund research that answers your second question. Dividing your research into multiple related projects presents you with a stronger budget narrative when you outline your research history in your funding applications.

Timelines can also be something to consider. Some applications have timelines that you can't meet in this funding round. Others have applications with lengthy review processes that may not fit your research goals. You will save time by reading the fine print carefully before commencing your application. Your obligations, should your grant be successful, are also embedded in the fine print. Some grants require monthly reports or a seminar presentation at the end of the grant. Others come with ongoing responsibilities that will have you working long after the grant has been completed (i.e., reviewing others' funding applications). Know what is required from you before you invest your time applying.

While you can successfully steer around many difficulties, if the aim of the grant application is different from your intended purpose (i.e., your grant funds research on the elderly and you are researching those in their midlife), or there are too many questions you can't answer, or you need to tweak too much of the wording to justify your budget, the grant is intended for a purpose that is not yours. You are wasting your time trying to complete it. It's time to search out other grants.[2]

Further reading

We know we have already recommended Khoo, Ward, and O'Donnell (2023) in our other pointers but we are going to do it again. Chapter 2 of Khoo et al. provides excellent advice on reading and understanding the motivations and expectations of funding bodies so you can shape your application accordingly.

Reference

Khoo, Tseen; Ward, Phil, & O'Donnell, Jonathan. (2023). *Getting research funded: Five essential rules for Early Career Researchers*. Routledge.

25. Crowdfunding your research project

Perhaps after searching for grants far and wide, there isn't anything that fits your immediate needs. Crowdfunding can present exciting opportunities for essential funds if you have good tech skills, like selling yourself online, or want to engage with potential donors about your research.

To be successful at crowdfunding, you are best to make a case that your research serves the public interest. Early career community-based research often falls into this category. Research outside the mainstream by unknown and emerging researchers can find crowdfunding support with the wider public. For example, niche groups such as women completing doctorates late in their careers may attract public interest.

When applying for crowdfunding an important consideration is any restrictions around funding targets. Some crowdfunding platforms refund donors if you don't reach the target and you can be left with nothing. Modest funding targets are most likely to succeed.

So how do you get started? Choosing your crowdfunding platform requires planning and preparation. You need to research independent and affiliated crowdfunding platforms. Some popular platforms are specific in their foci (i.e., science-focused platforms such as Scifund Challenge or socially conscious projects such as Chuffed.org). Others (such as Kickstarter) cater to a wider set of projects. In some instances, (i.e., Deakin University (Aust.)) universities have seen the value of crowdfunding and partnered with platforms such as Pozible.com.

When choosing among platforms that might work for you, it's important to read reviews by previous users. Check for any terms and conditions. When reviewing the fine print consider whether the platform is listed as a charity and whether it provides tax deductions for donors. Costs can differ. Some crowdfunding platforms have expensive fees and administrative costs. Conditions on when funds need to be spent also differ, as do platform security around transferring funds and protection of donor information.

Once you have chosen a platform, the next step is to design your webpage to appeal to your audience. Most platforms give plenty of advice on presenting your page and most have standard templates for you to fill in, with options for formatting tools, and importing images, videos, etc. Many allow you to customize your webpage to reflect who you are and the nature of your research. By bringing a little of yourself into your webpage, you help your audience share your passion. This can take some thought. Photos and videos on your platform are useful as they help 'sell' your project. Selecting and creating media for the platform can be time-consuming so think about how you might use your photos and videos for other purposes, such as a conference paper.

If you are thinking about offering something to your donors in kind, are you happy to give an acknowledgment in your future publications, or do you feel you want to give more (i.e., free copies of books, free seminars, etc.)? Promise only what you can realistically deliver.

Once everything is up on the platform, get your message to as many people as possible. To attract a wide range of potential donors who can locate the link to your page easily, tap into all your personal and academic networks. If you know people with many Facebook friends, ask if they can promote your crowdfunding initiatives. Or perhaps you could get public or institutional media coverage. University or organization newsletters can often advertise your initiative. Any third-party endorsements from academics or public figures widen your audience and give you more chances to reach your funding goal.

The platform isn't something you can leave unattended. It is crucial to regularly monitor your platform to check that everything is functioning as intended. Thank your donors, answer their queries, update the progress of your project (including incoming funds), and read any donor messages carefully. You might find that people or organizations interested in your project may want to continue associating with you after the project is completed. These contacts can become invaluable to develop further public interest in your work.

Another consideration is your timelines. While crowdfunding is often a faster way of securing funds than grant applications, it pays to be realistic about the length of time you want to devote to your crowdfunding initiative. 30–45 days is typically long enough to secure funding. Over time the donations stop trickling in.

There are a few last but important administrative things. Details about your funding sources need to be included in ethics applications and acknowledged in publications. If you are employed at an institution, there may be processes for receiving and distributing funds that you need to abide by, including letting administrative bodies know of any funding you receive. There is also the issue of how, and if, any crowdfunding can be listed on your institutional research profile. Contact the research office or your immediate supervisor for what you can and cannot list.

Further reading

Sauermann, Franzoni, and Shafi (2019) provide a comprehensive review of successful crowdfunding strategies. Wheat et al. (2013) highlight the potential benefits of crowdfunding for you, your research community, and your donors. They cover opportunities for public outreach, and its role in educating the public.

References

Sauermann, Henry; Franzoni, Chiara, & Shafi, Kourosh. (2019). Crowdfunding scientific research: Descriptive insights and correlates of funding success. *PloS One*, *14*(1), e0208384. https://doi.org/10.1371/journal.pone.0208384

Wheat, Rachel. E.; Wang, Yiwei.; Byrnes, Jarrett. E., & Ranganathan, Jai. (2013). Raising money for scientific research through crowdfunding. *Trends in Ecology & Evolution*, *28*(2), 71–72. http://dx.doi.org/10.1016/j.tree.2012.11.001

26. Writing your funding proposal so that it sells

Whether you are applying for a grant or crowdfunding your research, you need to sell your idea, and like other forms of research, this starts with a short snappy title. A reviewer of your grant application has limited availability to evaluate your proposal and decide on its outcome. A crowdfunding donor is unlikely to spend more than a moment looking at your site. Your title makes a difference.

Building a good title can be challenging. A shorter title helps to draw your reader in. Find out early about any word (or character) limits for your grant or crowdfunding platform before your heart is set on a title that might be too long. You might find it helpful to read the list of funded projects in past rounds of your chosen funding body or look at successful titles of crowdfunding sites. Notice how others have constructed their titles and subtitles and the keywords they use to connect their ideas. There might be a word or two that could be useful to lift your title.

Your friends and colleagues can often be a good source of ideas for snappy titles. You might toss ideas around over lunch. If you have a teaching position, your students might appreciate a chance to contribute title ideas for your research. You might consider a suggestion box outside your office where students (and colleagues) can drop you a note when they have an idea for a great title.

The abstract is the second item any reader sees, and it can make or break your chances of funding success. Your abstract provides the first details about your project. As a rule of thumb, explain what your idea is about first. If your abstract is 50 words, use your first sentence explaining your idea, if it is 100 words, you need two sentences, if it's 250 words, you need a short paragraph. In all instances, the initial words of your abstract must leave your readers convinced they understand your research. To check how potential readers might interpret what you have written, read the initial sentences of your abstract to your friends and ask them to explain what they think this part of your abstract means to them. If your friends can't paraphrase your basic idea, other readers won't fully understand your idea either. You can't sell an idea if your readers don't understand it.

Once your reader is aware of your topic, you need to convince your readers of the innovation or importance of your idea. You won't get funding if your readers can't see why they should fund you. When writing this part of your abstract, keep information about what is already known in the field to a minimum. There is ample space in the body of the grant application or on separate pages in your crowdfunding site to expand on how your work relates to other work in the field and to elaborate on your methodology. Methodological details in your abstract should likewise be concise. Think about whether you might summarize your chosen methods in a word or two (e.g., The study uses [*an ethnographic approach/a survey/interviews*] *to* bring to the fore [......]).

Finally, even if your research is blue sky (knowledge for knowledge's sake), a successful abstract mentions the future potential of any knowledge gained from your research. Could another researcher use any of your research outcomes, and if so, how? The greater the perceived value of your research, the greater your chance of selling your idea.

Once you have a complete abstract, remember that further refinement will improve it. Seek advice about how to improve your full abstract with everyone and anyone who will listen. If you have graduate students, you might share your abstract with them and ask if they can find a word that could be improved, a word that could be omitted, or even better, a clause that could be reframed. They might enjoy being the ones to give you advice for a change.

With the title and abstract sorted, you have set the stage for the rest of your proposal. In the introduction to the main body of your funding proposal, pay particular attention to your initial paragraph so that you do not cause any confusion. The content (and wording) of your initial paragraph must align perfectly with the content and wording of your abstract. Have your abstract handy when you write the first paragraph of your introduction. A little repetition in your initial paragraph (with some elaboration) can work effectively to consolidate ideas in a grant proposal. You need less repetition for crowdfunding because your overall text is much shorter.

Selling your research also means explaining how your research is to be done. Selling this part of your project shares similarities with selling your publications. Demonstrating that your methods are reliable and useful for the task at hand is necessary in every aspect of research (see Pointer 16 on writing for publication). If your methods are innovative, highlight this. To sell your project, there are a few extras in your proposal that require your attention. Your funding proposal must be able to communicate with diverse readers. Few of your readers will be members of your immediate field of expertise. In crowdfunding platforms, perhaps all your readers fall into this category. Restrict technical terms and abbreviations to a minimum as these can create reading difficulties for those outside your immediate field of expertise. To get ideas on restricting technical terms and abbreviations, peruse successful grant applications and crowdfunding platforms for useful insights into where and how specialized terms and abbreviations can be used.

Finally, selling your research also involves selling its people. Reviewers must be clear about why you and your research team should get the funding. Our next pointer focuses on putting you and your team into your application.

Further reading

Chapter 5 in Borkowski and Howard (2006) provides practical suggestions when applying for grants. We recommend it highly.

Reference

Borkowski, John G., & Kimberly S. Howard. (2006). Applying for research grants. In Fredrick T.L. Leong & James T. Austin (Eds.), *The psychology research handbook: A guide for graduate students and research assistants.* (2nd ed), pp. 433–442. Sage.

27. Writing yourself and your team into your funding applications

To be successful in your funding proposals, it is essential to write about yourself in positive ways to highlight what makes you special and why you have the requisite expertise to complete the research. Showing yourself in a positive but realistic light is a delicate balance. You can't be too boastful or too modest. Self-promotion can be hard work if it isn't something you enjoy.

Explaining your interest in the research topic is a great way to start. Write a couple of sentences or paragraphs about your (and your team's) passion for your research and why you and your team want to pursue it. Grab ideas from wherever you can. Perhaps you or a team member already have a paragraph about your passion for research in your work profile, or on one of your social media platforms (see Pointer 3). Or maybe you have the beginnings of a paragraph in one of your job applications.

Lived experiences help bring out your passion and demonstrate that you and your team are the right people to conduct this research. When writing about your lived experiences, remember that they come in different forms. Some are academic. You (or a team member) may have written a relevant literature review or a research article. Your doctoral thesis might be in a related area. Perhaps you or a team member has written a piece in a community newspaper or given an interview.

Perhaps someone may have written about you, your research team, or your research. Even one small comment can bring out the importance of your work, and reinforce an image of you as a capable, thorough, or innovative researcher. Perhaps you received feedback about your depth of knowledge from one of your thesis examiners. If you have published with anyone senior in the field, or you have had an opportunity to publish a chapter in an edited volume or write a journal article in a special issue with reputable editors and publishers, note this.[3]

If conducting community research, previous roles you have had in the community you are researching or any positive experiences with prior community research can bring your potential to the fore. If members of a particular research community have suggested that you complete this research, note this. If you can show that the community already believes in you and your team, crowdfunding donors and funding agencies will be inclined to trust you.

Whatever your experiences, write in ways that show relevance. Consider how what you and your team have done up to this point (or at least your most recent work) relates to the present project. Make this information short for crowdfunding, but it needs to be there. Most readers will not take the time to scrutinize your CV. If you like telling stories, try using this genre in your application to connect the pieces of your research narrative. Stories are a great genre for making connections.

If you are unsure and a bit nervous about writing research profiles, practice. Make a point of talking about your research to everyone you meet (see Pointer 4 on conferences for further details). Listen intently to how other researchers introduce their teams to pick up novel ideas, insights, and wording about how to promote yourself and your team in your funding initiatives.

While crowdfunding platforms need only a little information about you and your team, grants often need more details about your lived ways of knowing, being, and doing as a researcher. There are many things that you could write about. You may have used the proposed theory and methods outlined in your current grant application in your doctoral thesis. You or other members of your team may have published in the area. Some members of your team may have worked as a graduate assistant or research associate on a project that employed methods similar to those proposed in your project.

Leadership is also important. Finally, do you have ways of knowing, doing, or being that show leadership (potential)? You can draw on previous experiences: have you organized meetings, run a conference, conducted interviews, or led previous research teams (even if it was a team of two) that you can mention in your grant application? If you have held a small grant and hired even one person for one small task, you have something to write about. See Pointer 29 on managing grants for other ideas.

Finally, grant agencies want to be assured that you will deliver on your promises. What previous successes have you had in other grants (no matter how small)? For a grant, provide sufficient background information (i.e., How many prior small grants have you received? How many of these were competitive? How many were funded by external research agencies? Were any highly prestigious or difficult to get? Were you a lead or sole researcher, etc.?). As you outline your experiences, remember your overall narrative: What have you achieved? How did one grant help you build your ways of knowing and doing for another grant? Did you accomplish all goals in your previous grant(s)? Did you surpass any of them?

Further reading

Folk and Pequegnat (2011) provide insights into completing grant applications. Keep your reviewers in mind as you write.

Reference

Folk, Susan, & Pequegnat, Willo. (2011). Common mistakes in proposal writing and how to avoid them. In Willo Pequegnat, Ellen Stover, & Cheryl Anne Boyce (Eds.), *How to write a successful grant application: A guide for social and behavioral scientists,* 95–103. Springer. https://doi.org/10.1007/978-1-4419-1454-5_1

28. Preparing your budget

Getting the budget right is not easy, it takes time to develop and requires a lot of thinking to know what to include and how to write a narrative that justifies your costs. Don't expect to fully grasp every aspect of your proposed budget when you start. While it can help you use a budgeting app, it's important to remember that it can't do all the work for you.

It helps to start with the key categories in your budget. Common categories include staffing, equipment, data collection tools, data analysis tools, travel, website design, promotional materials, etc. However, each research project is unique and can have special expenses (i.e., gifts, translators, etc.).

If you can create your own budget categories design ones that allow you the greatest flexibility to move funds around when you need to. Here are a couple of examples. When considering travel costs, 'Transport' is a better budget category than 'car rental'. You may want to alter your plans at the last minute if flights to your research site come on sale or vice versa. Even your subcategories should be as broad as possible. For data analysis, a general category for coding and analysis is better than two separate categories as coding may take less time than you envisaged and analysis more time, or accessories (with examples which include microphones, batteries, etc) is better than an itemized list of equipment. It gives you more wiggle room to purchase a microphone stand if you suddenly need one and you haven't listed it in your budget.

Once you have designated the key budget categories, it's time to drill down into the details. Begin with budget items you understand more fully. For example, let's consider staffing, as this is a common category in many funding applications. Start with your ideal. What type of researchers and support staff would you prefer on your perfect research team? This might include research associates, post-docs, doctoral, or master candidates, or undergraduate students. It might also include a research manager, community gatekeepers, etc., or outsourced help (i.e., transcription services, statistical support, data entry, etc.).

Once you have a potential list of your ideal staffing, it's time to consider the tasks you need each to complete, the hours necessary for the core tasks and any associated tasks linked to the core task. For example, for a one-hour interview or focus group, include time to travel to the interview (with enough time to find parking) and set up for the event without running a sweat, time to explain the project and fill in consent forms, time to pack up and leave congenially, and time to travel back to the office. At the office, there needs to be time allocated for post-interview tasks such as labelling of interview data, proper storage of ethics documentation, the documentation of any pseudonyms and critical information about the interview context (i.e., the participant was distracted; one participant took over the focus group and perhaps unduly influenced the group responses, etc.). There also needs to be time allocated for interviewers to catalogue key aspects of the data (i.e., length of the interview, number of recordings, etc.). If support staff will be doing many of these tasks, interviewers need time to supply the relevant information to them. These tasks might only take a few minutes, but they quickly add up.

When considering administrative tasks, include ample hours for time-consuming tasks such as flyer preparation, staff and participant recruitment, and training. These tasks are often overlooked when planning a budget and usually take longer than expected. Include adequate hours for general administration to keep everything working smoothly and to ensure everyone gets paid on time. Check with colleagues about how much time general tasks should take.

Next, you need to consider what you can afford. If you have enough funds to match tasks with your ideal staff, that's great news. If you can't, consider how different staff configurations might affect your budget, and where you are willing (or not) to compromise. While it might be great to get your post-doc or interviewer to enter your data, if your budget needs to be trimmed, could this task be delegated to a research assistant? Do you need a doctoral candidate to conduct your interviews or focus groups, or could a member from the community work just as well (or better)? In focus groups, an extra person is handy to set up equipment so everything goes smoothly, and the interviewer can focus on the event. But can you afford this luxury? Perhaps an extra half-hour time allocated to setting up and a little extra downtime for one researcher may be all your budget can manage.

There are also employment contracts to consider. Is it more economical to hire a post-doc for three or four days a week and an undergraduate student for the other day(s) than to hire a full-time post-doc? To avoid costs associated with full time contracts, three part time research assistants may be more economical than one full time one. These decisions are not easy ones. Sometimes the cheapest option is not the most economical one. While a post-doc costs more than a doctoral candidate, and a doctoral candidate costs more than an undergraduate student, a researcher with more experience might do a better job and take fewer hours.

Costs around staff turnover are another issue to consider. Higher staff turnover means more recruitment and training. While doctoral candidates and post-docs might stay for the length of your project, part time research assistants may look for better opportunities before project completion.

The more important question may be: Do you have someone in mind who can do the job well and would you like to keep them on for the entire project? If so, work your budget around keeping that person on staff. To sustain staff morale, plan in the budget for increases in staff wages and the occasional bonus if warranted.

When you have finished thinking deeply about all the details for all items in your budget, what you need and what you can work around, and why, preparing and justifying your budget narrative will come naturally.

If you are floundering in all of this, workshops on budgeting can help. The organizers of these workshops have deep insights into organizing budgets and cutting costs. They also have specialized insights into local expectations (i.e., hours needed for tasks for your context). If they lack the specific information you need, they can probably point you in the right direction. They may even know of an experienced research assistant who can assist in your project, or a sample budget narrative that you might use as a template.

If you are an ECR who doesn't like to ask questions at these sorts of events, approach the organizer before the workshop starts and ask if there is time to discuss specific issues after the event. If not, convince yourself to speak up, or if the event is free, ask an outspoken friend to ask some of the questions for you.

Finally, it's important to remember that you are leading the project and ultimately responsible for it. This involves you keeping in mind your ways of knowing and doing. Decide what you can and cannot do. If budgets and accounts are 'not your thing', consider adding the necessary hours for someone to help prepare (or at least review) your budget. Your mentor an experienced researcher in your workplace, research office, or workplace accountant, can provide valuable advice.

Further reading

Browning (2022) is a useful resource for issues around grant applications. Chapter 18 of Browning's book offers a step-by-step process for preparing a budget for your grant application.

Reference

Browning, Beverly A. (2022). *Grant writing for dummies* (7th ed.). John Wiley & Sons.

29. Taking your project through to completion

You have written a successful funding application. You are now at the exciting (and challenging) part of executing your plan. The success of the project revolves around you. Now is the time to focus on you, how you can create a cohesive team, highlight your project's visibility, assess the ongoing status of the project, and prepare yourself for the unexpected.

Good team dynamics are essential. Working hours can make or break how teams work together and how work gets done. Start with you, as you are leading the project. Take stock of your regular working hours. Do you have a lifestyle that means you work long hours? Do you have childcare obligations that mean that you are not at work at certain times of the day? Your team members don't have to have the same hours as you, but they need to be able to connect with you, and find common ground, so tasks are done in the best way possible. How you organize your time depends on your management style, how well it works depends on your ways of communicating this information and negotiating where required.

When considering your team, consider the type of people you like to work with. Do you want experienced people well-versed in the tasks at hand, who can work independently and make on-the-job decisions when you are not around as long as they report these back to you. Or do you like to manage every small detail and need people who follow instructions to the nth degree?

Establishing your preferred medium of communicating is also important. Do you want to conduct most of your interactions with your team members online or face-to-face? Different situations call for different mediums. You need to be clear about what you want so everything flows smoothly. Any proposed changes are best given in written form, online, where they can be accessed on short notice.

No matter how well the team works together, things will go wrong at some stage. When this happens, it's important to remember that you are the boss. You need to have coping mechanisms in place. Ask your mentors for ideas. You might want to have a friend or colleague outside your team that you can talk with and help you blow off steam. You don't want to get angry around your team. See Pointer 50 for further details.

Whatever your management style, you need to set a positive example. A cohesive productive team thrives on gratitude. There are many opportunities to express gratitude. A simple thank you when team members question your ideas and generate new ones, when tasks are completed on time, or when team members stay behind to help support you when something unexpected goes wrong can work wonders for rapport.

Gratitude works well because it is contagious. If you express gratitude, your team members are likely to learn from you and express gratitude to others: to thank all those involved in their workings on your project, from the university librarian who may have aided in your literature search to the statistician who may have offered advice about statistical tests. A simple 'thank you' brightens someone else's day. It can also create goodwill for your research project if you need last-minute help in the future.

Other important steps to a successful project revolve around advertising your project. This typically begins with a website. Consider whether your workplace might host the website, or if you should invest in an independent server that can be transported elsewhere if you think you might change your physical or academic location midway through the grant or immediately afterward.

When designing your website, consider its appearance. You want your website to promote you, your team, and your project, help attract potential participants and secure future funding, but you also want one that is not cluttered. Get help to create a website that is easy to update and manage. This will save time, nerves, and in the long term, money.

At the beginning of your project, it is useful to remember that all you really need in a website is a homepage. Any homepage should contain the names; of you, your project, and your funding agency. You also need a concise highly readable description of the project, perhaps with a photo of you and your team or some other pertinent image. At the bottom of the page, add contact details (a phone number and email link) so you are contactable.

An additional page with information about team members, and their roles, with links to their academic credentials is another useful early step. Advertising each team member's roles sets the stage for aligning staff with specific tasks and lets everyone know when they need help. Remember to regularly update your website when members come on board, and when they leave.

Another key part of any successful project is keeping it on track. If you have a little leeway in your timeline, it helps to start with one small self-contained part of your project. Starting small allows you time to finetune your project and lets you see your team's strengths. This experience opens opportunities to find alternative ways of doing if what you planned isn't quite working out as you envisaged.

Regular meetings are essential to keep a project on track, no matter how busy you might be. Regular meetings help the team make small adjustments to the project as it progresses. You might convene short standup meetings for five minutes every week. Whatever you do, ensure decisions are based on a culture of encouraging questions. If you are proactive and listen intently, problems won't have opportunities to build up.

Successful projects also cope with change. One common one is changes in staffing. Who will design the questionnaires or survey instruments if the person you had in mind takes another job? Who will write (or help write) the ethics application, if the allocated researcher is suddenly sick? Who will conduct the literature review for a paper if interviews have been rescheduled and the allocated researcher is busy in the field? You don't want the answer to be 'you' in every scenario. Allocating time for team members to write up the processes involved in their tasks enables others to do those tasks if required. Updating these documents and keeping them in accessible places will save time even if no replacements are needed. Writing up pertinent details makes reporting time so much easier. Good record keeping is also vital for remembering the fine details about methods when composing manuscripts for publication written well after most of your staff have gone on to other positions.

Finally, when managing your team, remember that it could be 'you' who cannot do a specified task. You may have health, family, and or community concerns. Our lives are complex. A key part of any contingency plan involves documenting your tasks in enough detail for others to do them. If you are someone who finds documenting your tasks unbearable, ask your research assistant to follow you around for a day and take notes of what you do.

Further reading

Maunder (2021) reflects on big projects and teamwork. Chapter 8 in Thomas and Hodges (2010) contains a how-to guide for managing research projects. Chapter 11 in Russ-Eft et al. (2017) discusses how research paradigms affect perspectives about how data is interpreted and analyzed, and how these different ways of knowing can create potential points of disharmony among team members. Their book explores ways forward when team members are aware of and willing to explore differences in ways of knowing, being, doing, and communicating.

References

Maunder, Rachel E. (2021). Staff and student experiences of working together on pedagogic research projects: Partnerships in practice. *Higher Education Research & Development, 40(6),* 1205–1219. https://doi.org/10.1080/07294360.2020.1809999

Russ-Eft, Darlene; Sleezer, Catherine M.; Sampson, Gregory, & Leviton, Laura. (2017). *Managing applied social research: Tools, strategies, and insights.* John Wiley & Sons.

Thomas, David R., & Hodges, Ian H. (2010). *Designing and managing your research project: Core skills for social and health research.* Sage. https://doi.org/10.4135/9781446289044

Notes

1. If you work in a non-academic setting, you could ask your current employer if they would consider subscribing to a survey instrument. They may be willing to put out the funds for a quid pro quo. You could offer to help design an in-house survey. This type of task can help you finetune your questionnaire writing skills before you embark on your research.
2. When looking for grants, keep a lookout for scams. If you have suspicions about a possible grant, ask your research office before you begin your application.
3. If you use statements others have written about you (i.e., thesis reports), get permission before you put them in your application. This is especially important for crowdfunding, as the information you write is in the public domain.

You as a supervisor

Overview

This chapter explores your identity as a supervisor. The initial pointers in this chapter ask you to explore your ways of knowing, being, and doing so that you attract supervisees who align well with what you research and who you are as a supervisor. The pointers then turn to successful ways of doing supervision. These pointers consider how to set up successful supervision practices and explore how to work within supervision teams. This chapter ends with a pointer on how and when to discuss co-publication with supervisees and the pros and cons of this type of co-publishing (Figure 7.1).

Figure 7.1 How well can you align your research plan and potential research candidates?

30. Understanding you as a supervisor

Becoming a supervisor is a new identity. This means that you can craft it your way.

Your lived experiences will play a part in informing you about how you want to design your supervision. These include ways of doing you encountered during your doctoral journey that worked well for you. Some of these ways of doing are ones you encountered informally: perhaps listening techniques that your supervisor(s) used to encourage productive discussions or techniques your supervisor(s) employed when they formulated questions to elicit elaboration. These ways of doing might include regular routines for wrapping up sessions or summarizing the content of what was discussed.

Other decisions about your preferred ways of doing are informed by ways of supervision you experienced that irked you during your doctoral journey. If you had a supervisor who didn't give regular feedback or one who regularly cancelled meetings, you might go out of your way not to do the same. If you received feedback with a scant explanation about required changes, you may want to introduce new ways of doing with thoughtful informative comments.

Still, other starting points depend on the type of supervision you desire. Do you only want to supervise research candidates who align with your ways of knowing? Do you only want to supervise candidates working in your specific field with your preferred theories and methodologies? While your wishes may change, you need to know the type of supervision you are comfortable with, and perhaps even write this into your research plan. It will help you decide whether a research candidate is meant for you.

Another set of questions concerns your comfort levels around the preparedness of potential research candidates. What ways of doing would you prefer your research students to know before they start their studies? Do you need your supervisees to possess high levels of academic English? Are you willing to work with a candidate who needs to raise their level of writing to meet academic standards, or would this drive you crazy? How research capable do you need your research candidates to be before they begin their research journey? For example, is 'keen to learn' enough at the start? The answer depends on how much support you are willing to give.

Yet another key aspect of successful supervision is how your ways of being, doing, and communicating fit with those of your research candidate. Although all candidates are different, certain candidates are easier to work with than others. What are your 'make or break' ways of being and doing? Time management and organizational skills can be breaking points. Attention to feedback can be another. As you are unlikely to get every aspect you want in a candidate or discover vital information before you start supervising, it's important to consider your options. Is a tardy candidate, who tends to cancel meetings at the last minute but is organized when they arrive, better than one who is on time but comes relatively unprepared for the supervision meeting? Is a candidate who is prepared but has ignored most of your feedback better than one who has attended to some of your feedback, but not dealt with it systematically?

There are a couple of things that you can do to help get your best match. Reference letters can provide useful clues as to how candidates work if you read them carefully. Or you might prefer to find out for yourself. You could interview prospective candidates or email them questions before agreeing to supervise. This will let you know how quickly they respond, and how clear they are in their responses. You could even ask for a small rewrite of one section of their proposal or refer them to an author's work that they didn't mention in their proposal to see how they react to new ideas.

Remember to check their CV. If it has any publications, hunt them down and read them. If there is a master's or honors thesis available, skim it for readability and attention to detail. Is the literature review thorough and critical? A mistake could mean years of agony and regret. It doesn't hurt to ask your mentor or more experienced colleagues about their opinion if something doesn't feel right before you commit.

Although you will rarely find a complete match (nor will any two research candidates be the same), the clearer you are about what you are willing to accommodate, the easier it will be to narrow the choices before you. Your answers will be highly personal.[1,2]

Further reading

Dlaskova, Mirosa, and Murachver (2004) have created a list of the ten most important qualities and the ten most substantial shortcomings of research candidates. Ismail, Abiddin, and Hassan (2011) highlight how you can finetune and develop your supervisor identity. If you need support, Motshoane and McKenna (2021) describe the transition from doctoral candidate to supervisor through the metaphor of boundary crossing. They argue that supervision is a highly complex and delicate pedagogy that takes time to learn.

References

Dlaskova, Julie; Mirosa, Romain, & Murachver, Tamar. (2004). Supervisor perceptions of quality postgraduate research candidates. https://www.otago.ac.nz/__data/assets/pdf_file/0024/327471/supervisor-perceptions-of-quality-postgraduate-research-candidates-001461.pdf

Ismail, Affero; Abiddin, Norhasni Zainal, & Hassan, Aminuddin. (2011). Improving the development of postgraduates' research and supervision. *International Education Studies*, 4(1), 78–89.

Motshoane, Puleng, & McKenna, Sioux. (2021). Crossing the border from candidate to supervisor: The need for appropriate development. *Teaching in Higher Education*, 26(3), 387–403, https://doi.org/10.1080/13562517.2021.1900814

31. Choosing research candidates that build your research profile

Supervising is gratifying and exciting, especially when research candidates work in your research area. Before leaping in and taking the first opportunity to supervise, think carefully about how the proposed candidate adds to your long and short term research plans. When research candidates want to research in a direction that is different from yours, it doesn't build your research profile and can be a lot of work.

Supervision is best when there is an overlap between what you are researching and what a potential research candidate wants to do. You will be more interested in the research, more knowledgeable about it, and there can be greater chances of co-publication (see Pointer 7 on co-publishing). When a candidate approaches you, you need to be prepared: What type of research could a research candidate undertake to help you achieve your research goals sooner? Do you have a recurring question that reviewers of your manuscripts ask that a master's or doctoral candidate might pursue? Do you have a research project with too many working parts that a research candidate could undertake, if you agree to supervise them?

If you are looking for more than one research candidate to supervise, pause to think about how supervision topics might interact, and whether your supervisees might be able to support each other and work together. When topics overlap, your supervisees might be able to work together and learn from each other. You might even be able to run group supervision if this appeals to you.

So how can you attract your sorts of research candidates? One way is to compose your academic profiles in ways that provide information to research candidates about your supervision interests. In your institutional profile, add a couple of research questions you would like answered and explain why these are important for your research agenda. Add details into your profile about research methods you enjoy (and why you enjoy them) and thoughts about your theoretical approach and why it appeals to you.[3]

You may have a pool of already available potential candidates. If you teach subjects in a master's program and have developed a rapport with a student or two with the capacity and interest in doctoral research, you could quietly encourage them to continue their studies and ask them to consider you a potential supervisor.

Opportunities for supervision might present themselves at conferences. When you are at your next conference, search through the student presentations. If you are impressed, create an opportunity to chat with the presenter about their work and their interest in further study. Even if the presenter has no interest, these kinds of discussions are still good to have as they give inexperienced presenters confidence in their ideas.

To find research candidates, sometimes you need to reach out to others. Contact experienced researchers in your area of expertise (in and outside your institution) and ask if they have any available candidates. Many established researchers have queries from more candidates than they can handle. They might love the idea of forwarding good prospective candidates your way.

Finally, make sure that you are not missing out. What procedures does your department or school have for accepting PhD candidates? If applications are filtered through the central body, talk with the person responsible for assessing applications. Ensure they are aware of topics and areas of interest to you. Let them know that you are ready and willing to supervise. You may be off their radar.

Further reading

The online supervisor training program at Epigeum has a module on attracting suitable doctoral candidates. https://www.epigeum.com/courses/research/supervising-doctoral-studies-second-edition/

32. Setting up successful supervision sessions

Success! You now have your own research candidate.

To prepare, seek guidance. If you are an ECR who likes structured approaches to learning, you might like to attend every seminar and workshop available around supervision processes. If you prefer less structured ways of doing, ask if you can sit in on supervision sessions with more experienced supervisors. There are lots of useful bits to learn.

Successful supervision needs to start with ground rules. While it may sound tedious, ensure you spend your initial session covering obligatory milestones in the candidate's journey, so they know what is required. Another important discussion concerns rules around research. To save yourself headaches, explain clearly to your supervisees that they must inform you about all research work they embark on during their candidature. This ensures they do not automatically add your name to their conference papers, conference proceedings, book chapters, or journal publications if you have only helped them with the ideas or read and commented on their work or worse, you haven't heard anything about the manuscript. It is ethically questionable to publish if you did not make a substantive contribution to the work. Supervisee work may cause other issues. If the research is problematic, it can inflict damage on your academic reputation. Or if the work is submitted to a low tier journal, your institution may be unhappy. It is almost impossible to take your name off a publication once it has been published.

It's also important to consider data ownership. If a supervisee uses your data for their thesis, set rules around any publication early in the candidature, including any prior approval needed to use data to publish.[4] For your supervision to be off to a great start all parties need to know what to expect.

Other topics to consider in initial meetings revolve around you and your research candidate's ways of being and doing: how do you both like to work? You might need to be flexible and work around their ways of doing. They have lives outside of academia too! Negotiate meeting times and frequency, work, and feedback expectations. If your candidate asks you to supervise in unfamiliar ways (i.e., an online forum), you can say no if you feel it will disrupt your ways of supervision. If you are agreeable to trying something out, look for tutorials or ask around for a researcher who has tried this supervision technique to find out more before you agree.

There are other things that you can do to encourage mutual understanding. It helps to ask your research candidates about their prior learning. As a coursework student, how were lectures and tutorials organized? Were students encouraged to do readings apart from what was stipulated in their course outline? Did they have any flexibility in assignment topics? Did they feel they were permitted to talk freely in class and question assumptions or data? A research candidate from a cultural context you know very little about may have very different lived experiences and expect very different ways of being, doing, and communicating. As an example, some cultures expect students to always do as instructed, even when they disagree. This can be disastrous in a supervision session. Open communication does wonders for supervision if it starts early in the candidate's program.

Even when the research candidate comes from a similar cultural context as your own, it's useful to clarify the differences between teaching and supervising. As a supervisor, you will not always want to tell your research candidate what to read, what questions to ask, or even lead the discussion. If your research candidate starts with different expectations, there will be confusion all round.

It also helps to inform the research candidate early in their candidature about your ways of doing during supervision sessions. If you typically ask for clarification (to the nth degree), explain that sequences of questions that drill down into topics in great detail are the most important questions you ask during their candidate. This is not because you do not understand but rather because you expect your candidate to be able to think through every assumption and substantiate every claim they make.

Next is something that can occur after you have had a few sessions. If the research candidate has produced an honors or master thesis, ask if it would be okay to discuss how their thesis would need to be reworked if it were a doctoral thesis (i.e., there may be a need for a more extensive literature review, the methodology might need to be more detailed, terms more clearly defined, or the analysis more critical). If the candidate is ready for this discussion, an example of how they need to change their ways of thinking and doing in their doctoral thesis can give them a clear pathway forward. If your research candidate is not confident enough to discuss their own work, a discussion about a good master's thesis would achieve the same purpose.

Asking the right questions and setting the ground rules at the beginning of your supervisory journey sets you and the candidate up for success. The next pointer addresses co-supervision.

Further reading

Cardilini, Risely, and Richardson (2022) unpack the common mismatches in expectations between supervisors and doctoral candidates.

Reference

Cardilini, Adam P.A.; Risely, Alice, & Richardson, Mark F. (2022). Supervising the PhD: Identifying common mismatches in expectations between candidate and supervisor to improve research training outcomes. *Higher Education Research & Development, 41*(3), 613–627, https://doi.org/10.1080/07294360.2021.1874887

33. Successfully co-supervising

Many institutions insist that before an ECR takes on a principal supervision role they must first co-supervise. This is often a very successful strategy. You can learn about policy, expectations about supervision, and how to deal with any supervision that doesn't go as planned. You also learn a lot about teamwork.

When thinking about co-supervision, it helps to be proactive and look for team members you believe you can work well with. If you are working in the same department or school as one or the other of your PhD supervisors, you might approach them. You know how your supervisors like to work and what to expect from their ways of doing. If you are working in a new institutional context, look for senior colleagues who have ways of doing that you admire, and ask if you can join one of their supervision teams.

If you are approached to co-supervise on a team with a principal supervisor you don't know well, find out about their ways of doing before you agree. Ask them how they conduct supervision sessions, how often they meet with their research candidates, and how feedback is provided. If unsure, talk to colleagues who have been part of their supervision teams before committing. Due diligence pays.

When exploring whether to be part of a supervision team, each person's contribution to the team must be clear. Ask yourself if you are comfortable with what you are being asked to do. If not, offer possible areas where you might contribute before you agree to supervise. You may feel capable of mentoring in academic skills, methodology, or student wellbeing.

Some candidates need this support more than they need help with content. Ensure that your intended roles are conveyed to the candidate and the other members of the team, and put this in writing, even informally in an email. You may need this later if you are asked to supervise in other ways.

If you have ideas about ways that you would prefer supervision sessions to be run, ask if the principal supervisor is open to any of them. You might offer to commence discussion in one session, the principal supervisor in the next session, and the candidate in the third. You and the principal supervisor may like a set routine or make decisions from week to week. There will be times when certain members of the supervision team have more time to prepare and days when one team member would like to take more time during the session to pursue a particular angle. Ask if you and the principal supervisor can create a little time for a brief discussion before the research candidate arrives to set the agenda. The supervisory team needs to look prepared.

When you feel ready, you might like to complete a supervision session alone. The principal supervisor is not always available, and you need practice before this happens. If the principal supervisor agrees, remember to brief them later, perhaps as a short email summary of the topics and any issues. Ask if they can do the same for you. You won't always be available to attend every session. Good supervision means always staying in the loop. You want to avoid giving the candidate that supervision is anything but seamless.

Extra people may be asked to join a supervisory session (such as a panel chair) at candidature milestones. In these more formal occasions, if in doubt, talk to the other team members before the supervision session about any issues that need to be covered and the best way forward so that everyone is working toward a common goal. Raise potential points of contention before the meeting with the candidate. Sessions at candidature milestones are often stressful for the candidate and panel members want the candidate to be left with a clear message about how to move forward in their candidature. Doctoral and master's candidates have plenty to worry about, and you don't want to increase their anxiety.

Further reading

Kumar and Wald (2023) discuss workload issues of supervision generally, and more specifically, workload issues in co-supervision arrangements. Their focus on co-supervision workload is a rarely documented aspect of co-supervision. Wald, Kumar, and Sanderson (2023) provide a useful 'conversational tool' to facilitate transparent discussions on co-supervision arrangements and pedagogies for supervision teams.

References

Kumar, Vijay, & Wald, Navé. (2023). Ambiguity and peripherality in doctoral co-supervision workload allocation. *Higher Education Research & Development, 42*(4), 860–873, https://doi.org/10.1080/07294360.2022.2115984

Wald, Navé; Kumar, Vijay, & Sanderson, Lara J. (2023). Enhancing co-supervision practice by setting expectations in a structured discussion using a research-informed tool. *Higher Education Research & Development, 42*(3), 757–769, https://doi.org/10.1080/07294360.2022.2082390

34. Co-publishing with supervisees

Co-publishing with a supervisee is common in some disciplines and is relatively rare in others. Choosing the right candidate for any co-publishing adventure is critical for its success. Much will depend on how ready your research candidate is to publish and how well your ways of being and doing mesh together.

There are lots of reasons to co-publish, with benefits for all parties well beyond the publication. You have the potential for a great long-term co-authorship. Your research candidate benefits professionally. Publishing with a supervisor sends a strong message about the supervisee's research qualities. Supervisors do not publish with just any candidate.

When you co-author with a supervisee, they receive a special type of mentorship different from thesis mentoring. A successful journal article requires insights into the publication game and the editorial process. These useful ways of knowing enhance the probability of your research candidate producing future successful publications, ones that may or may not involve you.

Before you embark on co-publishing with a research candidate there are a few things to consider. The first question to ask yourself is: Does the candidate have the stamina to publish? It can take years to reach publication. Are they willing to continue with a publication if their goal is to work outside academia? The second question to ask is about resilience. Is the research candidate resilient enough to deal with the potential heartache of reviewer feedback and/or rejection? Not everyone can handle an extensive critique of their hard work.

A third concern is timing. When embarking on a potential publication with a research candidate, it is important to choose the right time to raise the idea. Where possible, any co-publication is best discussed toward the end of their candidature. During candidature, a supervisee is time poor. After thesis submission, the supervisee often has more time and energy to put into a publication. It is also easier to author a publication post thesis as you can see which parts of the thesis would make for a strong publication. You can also potentially move the manuscript in a slightly different direction from the one considered in the thesis (see Pointer 48 in Starks & Robertson, 2024).

While the best time to discuss co-publication with a research candidate is post-thesis, there are times when the idea of co-publication might be discussed earlier in the candidature. If a strong candidate has a wealth of rich ideas, and research questions, or has collected excessive data for a thesis, they might be more willing to let go of some aspects of their thesis if you offered to work with them on a post-thesis publication. This idea has multiple advantages: it can streamline the thesis direction, make the supervision easier overall, and help the research candidate complete their candidature on time. It will also legitimize your staking a claim in the publication and avoid any risk of appearance that you are publishing on your supervisee's shirttails.

Setting up ground rules is important. In your initial publication meeting with your supervisee, all parties must agree on who does what in the publication, and when. If you see your role in the publication as guiding, finetuning, and expanding your candidate's work, it is important to take time to explain how a journal article needs to be written. This is the time to explain why it isn't a good idea to start by cutting and pasting text from their thesis.

It's also important to explain your part in the editing process and how this might differ from that provided for the thesis. The thesis was their research work, the publication is theirs and yours, and there may be some instances where you propose that something be rethought. As you are mentoring and co-authoring, carefully explain the reasons for any suggested changes. If you explain clearly, you mightn't have to make similar edits later in another section of the manuscript, your co-author might do it on their own.

Roles post-submission of the manuscript also need careful consideration. If you see yourself as taking primary responsibility for the post-review revision process, explain to your supervisee how extensive any changes might be. Ask how they want to contribute to the editing process, so they don't feel excluded, and you don't feel that you are doing all the work.

Other considerations include co-authoring with candidates from less privileged backgrounds. This type of co-authoring has the potential to place the research candidate in a privileged position that can help them succeed in their career, and within their community. For this to work, they will need to bring their ways of knowing to the fore and perhaps seek community approval for you to be part of any publication. Points to discuss with them before you agree to co-author include: Can they handle a critique of their ways of knowing? Do they want to own access to their ways of knowing or allow you co-ownership of some of these ideas?

Think about your own reservations about others' ways of knowing. How comfortable do you feel with editing text where ways of knowing are embedded in the ways of communicating? Can you as an ECR follow and let yourself be led by others' ways of doing and communicating?

Finally, there are issues of first authorship. Is the first author the one who does the most work or the owner of the ideas? There are multiple authorship accreditation practices, and you need to find which is appropriate for each context.

Further reading

Haertling and Beach (2010) describe their successful co-authoring experiences as the supervisor and the doctoral candidate. Clowes and Shefer (2013) also share stories of co-authorship from the perspectives of candidates and supervisors. The latter work has a frank discussion of the political and ethical issues of co-authoring with doctoral candidates and gives valuable insight into the value of knowledge sharing.

References

Clowes, Lindsay, & Shefer, Tamara. (2013). "It's not a simple thing, co publishing": Challenges of co-authorship between supervisors and students in South African higher educational contexts. *Africa Education Review*, 32–47, https://doi.org/10.1080/18146627.2013.786865

Haertling, Amanda Thein, & Beach, Richard. (2010). Mentoring doctoral students towards publication within scholarly communities of practice. In Claire Atchison, Barbara Kamler & Alison Lee (Eds.), *Publishing pedagogies for the doctorate and beyond,* pp. 117–136. Routledge.

Notes

1. Identities are multiple, and you can perform more than one supervisor identity. Understanding diversity and difference is critical to good supervision.
2. It pays to be aware of rules and regulations. Rules may have changed if it has been a while since you completed your studies. Supervision rules and regulations differ across institutions. Attend a few supervision workshops to ensure that you understand expectations so that the advice you give your research candidate is good advice.
3. On your institutional profile, add links to your other social profiles (i.e., Google Scholar or ResearchGate). Research candidates are often keener to work with a supervisor if they know about their research.
4. A footnote ascribing the dataset to its appropriate owner or co-authorship might be warranted if your grant funds the research.

Difficulties

Overview

This chapter focuses on aspects of the ECR experience that don't go as planned and makes suggestions to help you move forward. This chapter begins with five pointers that explore key writing and publication issues. The pointers commence with the thorny issue of co-authorship strains and the time it takes to write before considering issues around the publication process: publishers' feedback, conflicting reviewer comments, and staying within word limits. Final pointers deal with disappointments in the grant application space, the dilemma of taking over from someone else's supervision, and challenges of team supervision (Figure 8.1).

Figure 8.1 Things don't always go to plan!

35. Your co-author(s) are driving you nuts!

Co-authoring is increasingly becoming a common practice, but it can be challenging. Tensions, disagreements, or breaches of trust can leave your wellbeing in tatters and leave you unsure how to resolve the situation. Things can go wrong when you address the issues and when you don't. Talking with your co-author when you are angry won't get you anywhere. If the run and hide option looks tempting, nothing will change. The first step is to determine the cause of your co-authorship tensions.

Often the problem centers around different ways of doing research. Authors work at different paces. Is your co-author too slow to get their part of the task done? Or are they pressing you to work faster? If this is the issue, the solution can be as simple as sitting down and discussing what works for each co-author. This may mean shorter deadlines for one co-author and longer ones for others.

It might not be ways of doing research but life events that cause issues. Perhaps all you need is to find out what is happening in your co-author's life and if there is anything you can do to help. If it is you who feels pressured and behind schedule (i.e., your workload might have suddenly increased), don't let embarrassment spoil a good co-authorship. All parties can adjust if everyone knows what the issues are.

Another common issue concerns different ways of approaching research. Discussions about how authors see themselves as writers and researchers reveal ways of being and doing that can help frame interactions. These ways can differ from one author to the next; in many cases, authors are unaware of alternative research methods that work well for others. Discussions about how you like to write can be illuminating for all concerned. As an example, if you like to drill down on issues in fine detail while your co-author needs to see the big picture first, it will be difficult to collaborate without this understanding. Specific foci for your meetings (i.e., the big picture in some meetings and the small details in others) can help move thoughts forward and help all concerned to better understand each other's writing process.

Another potential issue is mutual expectations about who does what. If it has become apparent that your expectations are not being met, then you need to have a discussion. It could be a simple misunderstanding, but it could be more. Co-authorship is often fluid. Unexpected events may mean one author appears to be taking on more than their fair share. If this is the case, it may be time to discuss changing the order of potential authorship. If you wait until the project finishes it is too late.

Mutual expectations about authorship can be tricky when there are power dynamics. If a senior researcher has different expectations, seeing their role as one of mentoring as a form of co-authorship without doing much (or any) of the writing, friction is likely. These expectations about co-authoring may be incompatible with yours. How you deal with this will depend very much on who you are. You might ask for a meeting to consider whether your co-author is prepared to make adjustments. They might be happy with your suggestion. Alternatively, you might want to bite your tongue and continue the project but take this as a lesson to clarify co-authoring expectations more clearly in the future. Another option is to tell your co-author that this is not how you wish to proceed and that you want to stop co-authoring with them. Don't rush into this as a solution before you think through any potential repercussions. You don't want to be in a position where you feel exploited, but you also don't want to lose a potentially good publication. It can help to have an informal discussion with your manager to forewarn them of the problem so that if formal action is required later, they are aware of the issue and can be more supportive. As a very last resort, if you think it best to go solo on the publication, every institution has dispute processes. If you can, appeal before publication. Before acting on this, think carefully about the consequences. A formal appeal can create unwelcome tensions when interacting with your colleague in other workplace contexts and run the risk of an unhelpful reference for your next job. Before offering you a position, many potential employers make informal queries to those they know before they make new appointments.

Co-authorship strains can also be tricky when you are in a position of power. If you are co-authoring with a student or supervisee, it might not go to plan. If your student or supervisee is not undertaking the work previously agreed upon, ask if they are still interested in the project. They may not be as keen as you thought or may have lost interest when they realized how much work was involved. If they are still interested, perhaps ask if you could do more to speed up progress. If you are struggling to keep your side of the deal, maybe you need to suggest changing your role from co-author to advisor. They can give you an acknowledgment in the article if this is warranted. If your student requires this publication to graduate, seek advice from a senior researcher about ways to get the writing moving along. Perhaps your expectations are too great. When publishing with a student, your role as a teacher/supervisor must come first.

There are times when the relationship between co-authors is more equal, but it still doesn't work. Some people can be the best of friends but can't work together. Conversations can be tricky if your co-author is a co-worker or friend. If problems persist after a frank discussion, consider the relative importance of the personal relationships vis-à-vis your project and excuse yourself from the project if you feel your friendship or working relationships are likely to suffer. Some research projects come at too great a cost. Some projects are best terminated for everyone's wellbeing. Having one less publication on your CV will not break your career.

At times, issues are bigger than the project. If you genuinely feel exploited, seek advice from other trusted senior researchers, your manager, or if that doesn't work, you could take it to the union. If your co-author's behaviour is socially or physically inappropriate, report it. It may not be easy for you but stick to facts and do your best to keep your emotions in check.

Further reading

Bozeman and Youtie (2016) focus on successful co-authorship and tackle the concerns of who is given credit and who might be left out. Gelman and Gibelman (2014) unpack what is causing the rise in co-authored works. Yeo and Lewis (2019) discuss the emotional side of co-authoring and what can make or break co-authoring relationships.

References

Bozeman, Barry, & Youtie, Jan. (2016). Trouble in paradise: Problems in academic research co-authoring. *Science and Engineering Ethics*, *22*, 1717–1743, https://doi.org/10.1007/s11948-015-9722-5

Gelman, Sheldon, R., & Gibelman, Margaret. (2014). A quest for citations? An analysis of and commentary on the trend toward multiple authorship. *Journal of Social Work Education*, *35*(2), 203–213, https://doi.org/10.1080/10437797.1999.10778960

Yeo, Marie, & Lewis, Marilyn. (2019). Co-authoring in action: Practice, problems and possibilities. *Iranian Journal of Language Teaching Research*, *7*(3), 109–123, https://doi.org/10.30466/ijltr.2019.120739

36. Your manuscripts take too much time to write

Whether co-authored or solo-authored, preparing a manuscript for publication can be a tortuous enterprise if your manuscript isn't going to plan, and a bit of panic has started to creep in.

Your manuscript can easily get held up if you are unsure about the direction of your manuscript or subconsciously feel that something is not right, but you are not sure what it is (or perhaps how to solve it). This can make you feel you are losing control.

It's time to communicate your ideas with others. Have a coffee or drink or walk with a colleague who understands your research. Be honest about what you have done and how you feel. To get a different perspective, quiz them about what they would do if they were conducting similar research. This may not always provide you with 'your' solution, but a thread in their argument can often prompt you to move your ideas in a slightly different direction.

You may be stuck on a section of your manuscript. If this is the case, it can be helpful to stop thinking about the entire manuscript and focus only on the bit causing you concern, as if it were a complete piece.

If your literature review is the problem, think about each part of your literature review systematically, paragraph by paragraph. Is every part equally current? Is every part presented in the most appropriate order? Does every paragraph contribute to your argument in the best way possible? By unpacking paragraphs, you see the manuscript in a different light, and this can often be the source of new ideas.

If your methodology is stymying your progress, try giving a departmental seminar about the pros and cons of your procedures. Talking about your work gives clarity. The audience can also be useful for spinning new ideas. Alternatively, you can work through the process on your own. If you are unsure if you have sufficiently justified each part of your procedure, try listing what you did and checking this list against what is written in each paragraph. Alternatively, you could recreate the methods in your head, take notes, and compare those notes with your written text.

If later bits of your manuscript are causing you concern, it's time to deconstruct the main point of each paragraph. Often when you write, your main point drifts a little. Perhaps you have a paragraph containing bits of earlier thinking, or your paragraphs are ordered in ways that no longer strengthen your work. Maybe you have one or more interesting and informative paragraphs, but these are now off-topic and should be deleted. Once you have your findings, discussion, and conclusion in place, return to your abstract and introduction to ensure that any claims are strong and convincing, and repeat the basic message in your findings, discussion, and conclusion. If you don't have a consistent main point throughout your manuscript, your reviewers won't be able to follow your train of thought.

You might be stuck but it has nothing to do with the manuscript. Whether you are writing a book or a journal article, writing by yourself, or co-authoring, you might be feeling time pressures. You can't make more time, so the only option is not to dwell on running out of time but to manage your time as efficiently as possible. Steady progress is better than boom and bust cycles.

When finding the best time to think, consider your ways of being and doing. Do you find it easy to pick up inconsistencies in your writing first thing in the morning or perhaps after the kids are in bed? If preparing your manuscript is a high priority to progress in your career, try to develop a schedule that embargoes your productive writing times. It's amazing how organizing your day a little differently can create clarity of thought (see Chapter 9 for dealing with publications for your CV).

Perhaps it isn't time, but something else external to you: a lack of support at home, your co-author, or your work responsibilities.

If everything in your manuscript seems OK, perhaps the issue is you. You need to believe in yourself as a writer. Joining a writer's group might give you the support you need. A writing retreat might help consolidate your thinking about who you are as a researcher and why the topic you are writing about is important. Talking in these forums can help consolidate your ideas, give you positive vibes to continue writing, and spur you on. These forums also help you frame a narrative about who you are as a writer and researcher which can guide you to construct your current manuscript and those in your future writing journey.

Another issue that might center around you is perfectionism. No manuscript is ever perfect. Give the manuscript to a trusted colleague (perhaps a critical friend who provided feedback on an earlier version of the manuscript) and ask them to provide you with a clear message about whether the manuscript is ready to submit. If you get positive feedback, submit it. If this makes you anxious, perhaps ask your friend if they can be in the room when you press the submit button. They could even press the submit button for you and they can celebrate with you afterwards.

There are times when a project goes nowhere, and nothing works. If there is no immediate way forward, it is time to stop this project. Not every manuscript makes it to completion.

Further reading

Ahmed and Güss (2022) provide general advice for addressing writer's block. If time management is your bugbear, Chapter 3 in Carter, Guerin, and Atchison (2020) explores productive writing strategies. While this work is focused on doctoral dissertation writing, there is ample food for thought about how your ways of being and doing as an ECR affect your writing practices. Janke, Wilby, and Zavod (2020) focus on important connections between your emotional health, successful writing, and the struggles researchers often experience when writing manuscripts.

References

Ahmed, Sarah, J., & Güss, C. Dominik. (2022). An analysis of writer's block: Causes and solutions. *Creativity Research Journal, 34*(3), 339–354, https://doi.org/10.1080/10400419.2022.2031436

Carter, Susan; Guerin, Cally, & Aitchison, Claire. (2020). Managing productivity. In *Doctoral writing: Practices, processes and pleasures,* pp. 51–91. Springer Singapore. https://doi.org/10.1007/978-981-15-1808-9

Janke, Kristin K.; Wilby, Kyle John; & Zavod, Robin. (2020). Academic writing as a journey through "chutes and ladders": How well are you managing your emotions? *Currents in Pharmacy Teaching and Learning, 12*(2), 103–111, https://doi.org/10.1016/j.cptl.2019.11.001

37. The review process is taking forever

Once you hit the button to submit your manuscript, the waiting starts. The online submission process allows you to track the ongoing status of your manuscript, but the wait can still be excruciating.

Like everything else in life, sometimes journals get behind schedule. If there doesn't seem to be any movement on your manuscript after three months, send a polite email to the editor to check on the status of the manuscript. They can tell you why your manuscript has been held up. Knowing where you are in the process can ease any anxiety and let you plan potential revision times into your writing schedule.

If there is no movement on your manuscript it may be because the editor has difficulties finding enough reviewers. Should this be the issue, ask if you can recommend several researchers in your field.

Another potential stumbling block in the review process is the time it takes for the editor to make a final decision about your work. Once your manuscript is back from review, the editor must decide whether to accept your work, ask for revisions, or reject it entirely. Each decision must be supported with evidence in their email response to you. If there is a difference of opinion between the reviewers, the editor may need some time to consider a response. If the online submission link states that your manuscript is back to the editor, let sleeping dogs lie as any attempt to push for an early response at this stage could work against you. The editor is busy with many other manuscripts, and it is much easier for the editor to reject your manuscript than to find a way for you to rework it. While you are waiting, get started on your next project. The more work you have underway, the greater your sense of empowerment.

The wait may simply be too long, and the editor may not respond to your emails. If it has been a year since you submitted it, this wait should not be tolerated. You should consider submitting it to another journal. If this is how you want to proceed, as a courtesy, explain that the process is taking too long. Should you decide to submit a future manuscript to that journal, the journal editor might remember your polite email and work to expedite your next manuscript.

If you submit elsewhere, you will have to start afresh but hopefully, the change in publication outlet will expedite things. Don't be tempted to resubmit without first revisiting your manuscript. Carefully review your work. There is always a sentence or two that could be improved and after this hiatus, picking up inconsistencies in your manuscript is a lot easier. Finally, don't rush through the new journal guidelines, they need your full attention. They demonstrate to the editor that you have purposely targeted your manuscript to their journal.

Further reading

The peer review process is a strong gatekeeper mechanism for research rigor. However, it is not without its critics. Brezis and Birukou (2020) delve into multiple issues with the peer review process used to assess manuscripts for publication. As the review process is a voluntary service, reviews can differ in quality. Some academics take their job very seriously and are highly diligent in their feedback, while others are not so much. Brezis and Birukou (2020) also provide an informative critique on the 'homophily' involved in the review process in which accepted ideas and formats are preferred, and anything radically different has a higher chance of being rejected.

Reference

Brezis, Elise S., & Birukou, Aliaksandr. (2020). Arbitrariness in the peer review process. *Scientometrics, 123*(1), 393–411, https://doi.org/10.1007/s11192-020-03348-1

38. Conflicting reviewer comments

You have finally received an email with the news about the status of your manuscript. You open it and are overjoyed to find a positive response from the editor, with one proviso – you do some further work and resubmit.

As you read through the feedback, your joy quickly turns to dismay. You discover that one reviewer thinks your manuscript is amazing, the other thinks it's complete rubbish and the two others sit in between! Take heart, you are not alone! Go for a walk, breathe, or perhaps even yell a little. Then go back and read through the comments again.

When you read this time, remember that reviewers place importance on different things and have different opinions about what they read. They see the world differently. In most instances, if a reviewer ignores an issue, it doesn't mean you should.

Often, the way forward is in a letter from the editor. A good editor will advise on what they think are the main issues you need to address. They may leave it up to you to decide among the available options. Ask for advice from more experienced colleagues, your supervisors from your doctoral studies, or a mentor. They have experience dealing with conflicting reviews.

Let's consider a few common scenarios of conflicting reviewer comments so that you can get a clearer picture. One reviewer says one part of your manuscript needs to be expanded, and another wants it deleted. This is often a case of not providing enough detail. One reviewer may have been able to piece together your thoughts, while the other may not have been able to do so. A reviewer who thinks (but is not sure) that they understand what you are trying to communicate will ask you to clarify what you mean, while a reviewer will likely ask you to delete what they don't understand. If you believe your point is vital to your argument, clarify its importance in the manuscript (in more detail than requested) and explain why your point is essential in your letter to the editor. If the contested point adds interesting and informative content but distracts from your main argument, concede that it doesn't fit in this manuscript, delete it, and move on. It's okay to admit that a point in your original manuscript is not useful. You can thank the reviewer for their insight in your response to the editor.

A particularly difficult challenge is when one reviewer critiques your theoretical and methodological underpinning. In most instances, if a reviewer is having difficulty understanding why you chose a theory or method to explain your data or answer your research questions, they may try hard to offer you another solution from a theory or method they know well. Consider their solution carefully. If it takes the manuscript far outside your comfort zone, will a revised manuscript in this direction still fit within your brand? If not, try enhancing the readability of your original argument for those outside your niche audience, explain arguments in greater detail, write the editor the most convincing argument you can, and take your chances. A detailed explanation goes a long way. If your revision isn't accepted, you still have an improved manuscript to send elsewhere.

Conflicting reviews can be frustrating and difficult to get your head around. These often center around the organization. Reviewer A sees the logic behind your organization and reviewer B can see neither rhyme nor reason to it. Sometimes reviewer B's suggested reorganization would do wonders for your manuscript, sometimes not. Rather than turning your argument upside down to appease a reviewer, first, consider adding a couple of sentences in the introduction to your manuscript and in key points further along in the manuscript to explain why you have organized the manuscript as you have. Look over your topic sentences in key paragraphs to check that they send the right message and then read each of your paragraphs carefully. There might be a sentence that sends the wrong message. that is easy to fix. If the flow in the revised text is better than in the original, your revised manuscript will have a good chance of success.

Once you have found solutions and have revised your manuscript, you need to write a response to the editor outlining what you have done and why. When detailing your revisions to the editor, be open to conflicting reviews and check that you have detailed every major item. This is critical to your success. There are several ways to do this. Some editors suggest that you present your revisions as a table, or through tracked changes. Others may prefer a letter. Small typographical issues can be listed together and noted as completed, without explanation.

When composing your letter to the editor, keep your tone conciliatory and respectful. The reviewers are members of your field. They have spent time carefully reading your work and have suggested improvements. Your response shouldn't ignore or dismiss their hard work. They reviewed your manuscript as a service to the research community and likely completed this task outside their regular work hours. If you are still reluctant to write a nice letter, keep in mind that your reviewers are usually sent a copy of your response, and they will be able to identify you if your manuscript is accepted in this, or if they look, in another journal.

Reviewer comments might have made you reconsider your manuscript. After rereading your manuscript in light of your reviews you can no longer see value in what you have initially proposed. Other times, the required changes take your manuscript well away from a narrative you are comfortable with. Or you may not have the data available to answer the questions the reviewers pose. If you feel this is the case, reply politely to the editor explaining your decision. It is good to have closure.

Further reading

Johnson (1996) describes the perennial stresses of addressing reviewer comments and has an excellent table that distills issues around conflicting comments. The title of Starbuck's article (2003) *Turning lemons into lemonade*, indicates his approach to addressing conflicting comments. His golden rule (No reviewer is ever wrong!), advocates a positive attitude that is well worth adopting when dealing with reviews.

References

Johnson, Suzanne Hall. (1996). Dealing with conflicting reviewers' comments. *Nurse Author & Editor*, 6(4), 1–3.
Starbuck, Wiliam H. (2003). Turning lemons into lemonade: Where is the value in peer reviews? *Journal of Management Inquiry*, 12(4), 344–351, https://doi.org/10.1177/1056492603258972

39. Your revisions exceed mandated word (or page) limits

You've tackled all the revisions and are happy with the result. This is exciting, but the changes have pushed you over the word limit. There are a few things that might help.

Before you panic, first recheck what is included in the word count. You might find embedded in the 'Instructions to Authors' helpful notes that you need. Perhaps there is a statement that says that references, footnotes, and appendices are not included in the word count. If this doesn't appear anywhere, check the wording in the Authors Guidelines carefully for other forms of leniency. In Instructions to Authors many journals and book publishers clarify the word limit (i.e., manuscripts must not exceed 10%). The statement on word limits might contain adverbs such as *ideally*. In these cases, your manuscript can contain another paragraph or two without worry. If there is nothing of this sort, and you have been asked to make extensive additions to your original manuscript, contact the editor to ask for some leeway but don't expect more than 10% extra as most editors have limited scope to bend the space rules, but it can't hurt to ask.

In most instances, it is you who needs to control the number of words in your manuscript. In most cases, you can meet the requirements if you try hard enough. Usually, editing your text (while frustrating) has benefits. It improves the readability of your manuscript. It is time well spent.

How you edit ultimately depends on your ways of being and doing. Some ECRs like to go systematically through their entire manuscript for superfluous words. These include unnecessary adverbs (e.g., very, too), repetitive sentences, or paragraphs that could be simplified, reduced, and combined into one. Alternatively, you might be an ECR who can't face the tedium of going through the entire manuscript. You might find it more productive to target specific parts of your manuscript. If you have superfluous findings, these might be shortened, or some even deleted. If you are an ECR who likes to provide long lists of references in your literature review, you might consider culling a few of the older or less relevant ones. It's amazing how many words you can cut out of a manuscript by deleting non-essential references.

Alternatively, you might try free writing. When you rewrite a paragraph or section from memory, you omit things. By comparing your two drafts you may find that it helps to evaluate the necessity of information in your text.

If you do this, don't be alarmed if your rewriting means that you added a few extra words. If adding a few additional words increases readability, it's worth it in the end. There will be other places where words can be deleted.

For those ECRs who enjoy editing, you could approach the word count as a game. Try to cut five words out of each paragraph. Once you get in the rhythm, you will be surprised at how easy it is to delete articles such as 'the' and 'various' and rearrange and combine sentences (i.e., the sentence 'This process is both frustrating and complicated' becomes to the noun phrase 'a frustrating and complicated process). You don't need to have absolute rules for editing. If you remove seven words from the first paragraph, perhaps three is good enough for the next (for tips for fine-tuning your writing see Chapter 5 in Starks and Robertson (2024)).

If you find editing the entire text looking for unnecessary words tedious, just open the manuscript to a random paragraph and start there. Then do another random paragraph. You don't have to scrutinize every paragraph or even track which paragraphs you have completed. If you go through the same paragraph twice, you might find it more difficult to delete words, but it may not be impossible. The advantage of editing in this way is that you are reducing the word count and improving the flow of your paper at the same time without the need to think about content.

If you still have a lot of extra words to delete and nothing seems to work to reduce your manuscript to the needed length, it's time to ask for help. To start you need to consider the type of help you want. Do you want someone to help with extraneous words? Experienced writers can easily spot opportunities for rewording or restructuring a paragraph or section. If this doesn't work, are you comfortable asking a colleague to recommend major edits? Having labored over your words for some time, you might find some of these recommendations confronting. They may suggest that you remove a point completely from your manuscript. If the point was important to you, this may mean that you need to go through the entire manuscript to take out bits of text from the introduction where you explain why this idea is important; from the literature review where you inform your readers about prior work in this area; in the findings that report on the data and in the discussion and findings. There may even be a sentence or two in the conclusion where you show its relevance. It's important to remember the end game is to get your manuscript published.

Bold ECRs might be willing to submit a revised manuscript that is over the word limit. If this is the case, it helps if you explain to the editor that your attempts at editing have reduced the word count, but not to the requirements. Sometimes this works, sometimes it doesn't. Whatever approach you take, review your manuscript carefully to ensure it still has coherence. It's very easy to edit out an important point or insert a typo or two into the manuscript when editing.

If the above editing options are not where you want to go, search for a different journal that will accept a longer manuscript.

Further reading

Gerring and Cojocaru (2016) challenge the idea of journals having short word limits, arguing that this approach does not serve disciplines well and that word limits constrict rather than enhance scholarly research. While their article does not help with culling words, they do show that you are not alone. There are good reasons why cutting words out of your manuscript leaves you feeling frustrated.

Reference

Gerring, John, & Cojocaru, Lee. (2016). Arbitrary limits to scholarly speech: Why (short) word limits should be abolished. *Qualitative & Multi-Method Research*, *14*, 2–12, https://doi.org/10.5281/zenodo.823308

40. Your grant application was not accepted

With fierce competition for limited available grant funding, not every grant application is successful. While pointers on successful grant proposal writing might increase your chances of success (see Chapter 6 for suggestions), you won't always be successful no matter how good your application is. So, what can you do to increase your chances of a successful application next time?

First look for any useful feedback. If there was no feedback, you could email the chair of the review panel to see if you can get more information. If you were given advice but didn't fully understand what was meant, show your feedback to your mentor and/or a critical friend. They can help clarify comments that don't seem to make sense to you.

One of the best ways forward is to be brave and move beyond the comments. Show your unsuccessful application to a researcher in your area who has had grant success. Don't feel embarrassed. They have had unsuccessful grant applications too. In your discussion, ask for critical feedback. The feedback you received from the panel doesn't cover all potential content changes. Ask them about how they would evaluate your application and what aspects of it would make them consider knocking back your application if they were reviewing it. If you can't bear to show a colleague your work, ask the research office for critical feedback on your application. Your feedback will likely focus on the following.

Your application may be strong, but it doesn't focus strongly enough on the grant's funding priorities. Check the grant's priorities and look for stronger ways to construct your application to work within the grant's priorities.

The problem may be the way you phrased parts of your application. Perhaps you might benefit from a catchier title and stronger claims in your introductory paragraph about why your proposal is innovative or important and meets the goals of the funding grant. Perhaps you need more explanation about why your chosen theoretical approach, methods, or more emphasis on your team's knowledge and suitability for the research. You might want to reread our pointers on grant success. Embark on any rewriting early so you have time later to tweak the application to meet word limit requirements.

Your application might benefit from a substantive change in content. Could another theoretical framing help your application? Would a change in methodology improve your application? Changing your theory or methodology can require adding another team member with this expertise. If this seems the way to go, start your search for an additional researcher as early as possible. You might add them to a small existing project to show prior work together. You don't want your application to look like you just added a new team member to make the application look better.

If you decide that a change in theory or methods would improve your chances of grant success, this decision may require other ones. Not everyone on the team needs to have a continuing role. Although it is difficult to let people go, you may need to restructure your team. If this is your plan, to keep goodwill, do this sooner rather than later. Search out colleagues with a strong record of grant success, a mentor or critical friend to help you find ways to structure conversations about letting members of your original research team go. These conversations won't be easy for anyone.

The budget may have been the source of your downfall. If you did everything we suggested in the pointer on budgets (see Pointer 28 for details), perhaps the detail wasn't the problem. Sometimes it is the amount that has failed you. If you need a large budget to cover the costs of your research and other researchers need far less, the funding agency may have decided that they can get more value by funding two applications than one. Another issue with grants with big budgets is their do-ability in the time limits. Research often takes longer than anticipated. If the funding agency has any doubts about your project, they won't fund you. In your next application, consider how much funding you need to do part of your project well, and how much you can realistically achieve in the allocated time. Getting a grant to cover one part of your original proposed project may give you more success. You don't need to do everything all at once.

Further reading

Koutsantoni (2009) gives insights into the structures of funding bodies and how to make them work for you. This work provides tips on the language of grant writing. Westra and Fleuren (2022) contextualize the disappointment of rejection and demonstrate that the initial rejection can be simply advice 'No, not this way'! Rather than a 'No, not ever'!

References

Koutsantoni, Dimitra. (2009). Persuading sponsors and securing funding: Rhetorical patterns in grant proposals. In Maggie Charles, Diane Pecorari & Susan Hunston (Eds.), *Academic writing: At the interface of corpus and discourse*, pp. 37–57. Continuum International.

Westra, Daan, & Fleuren, Bram. (2022). To come, to see, to conquer: Practical pointers in applying for funding and securing your initial grants. In Dominika Kwasnicka & Alden Yuanhong Lai (Eds.), *Survival guide for early career researchers*, pp. 119–129. Springer International.

41. Your grant got reduced funding

Lucky you, you got funding! Your problem is that the amount is far less than you budgeted for in your application. If you have already cut the budget to the bone in your original application, reducing your budget further can be daunting and leave you in utter despair.

While your first reaction to any reduced funding might be to return the grant to the funding agency, it isn't the best choice. A major grant establishes you as an ECR and sets you up for publication and promotion.

The question you need to ask is: how can you make your research viable with these reduced funds? You have three basic options: reduce your expenditure without diminishing the quality of the research or the outcomes; reduce the objectives of the grant; or find more money elsewhere.

You can often reduce expenditure if you think laterally. To save a little on staffing (check Pointer 28 for further staffing options), could you hire a transcribing firm to do a rough transcript? These services aren't perfect, but they are quick and relatively cheap. You could overview the transcripts and listen selectively to the recordings, editing only those bits of the transcription you are interested in for your analysis.

To save a little on travel, could you run fewer trips for data collection with more interviews each time or perhaps conduct some interviews online? Could you space your interviews out so you can safely return home after a day of conducting interviews rather than spending funds on accommodation? If you need to stay overnight, could you possibly stay with a friend? Could your team forego a conference away and attend something local, or if you feel you need to attend the international conference in your field, could you send only one team member?

To save on equipment, could you rent rather than buy? Is it possible to borrow? Colleagues may have excess equipment from their grant and administrators have surplus equipment tucked away in cupboards. Consider what you and your friends own. Could personal smartphones have sufficient sound and video recording for your research purposes? To save on gifts, where you might have hoped to offer participants small gifts, could you offer in-kind gifts (see Pointer 22 on working with communities)?

When reducing your budget doesn't work, you can turn to reducing the project itself. What is essential to conduct the research? Are there ways of still fulfilling your research objectives while reducing costs? Could you conduct fewer interviews or focus groups without jeopardizing the quality of your research? Could you do less data analysis? Could you focus on one research question rather than two? Could you leave an aspect of your research for a later project? Grant agencies often allow flexibility to reduce the scope of your project if your budget has been reduced.

A third option is to look for additional funding. Might your department or school have a departmental research assistant you could borrow to conduct some of your research? You won't know if you don't ask. Could your manager let you use their stationery and internal mail to send any mail or parcels that cannot be sent electronically? Perhaps there are small internal grants that you could apply for to cover the gap? Perhaps you could sequence your research. Maybe you could forge ahead with an interview, questionnaire, survey, or focus group that answers one of your research questions and then do a follow-up (with a subset of the same or other participants) about other research questions if and when you have secured additional funds. In the meantime, your existing grant gets you started on your research. Sequencing your research has the advantage of picking up potential glitches in your methods that you can improve.

If you are having emotional difficulty finding options to help you meet your new budget requirements, the research office at your research institution (if you have one) can help. There are people in the research office who specialize in budgets.

Further reading

Lawes, Schultz, and Eid (2020) consider how to conduct solid valid research without necessarily using all gold-standard practices.

Reference

Lawes, Mario; Schultz, Martin, & Eid, Michael. (2020). Making the most of your research budget: Efficiency of a three-method measurement design with planned missing data. *Assessment, 27*(5), 903–920, https://doi.org/10.1177/1073191118798050

42. Your principal supervisor is causing you headaches

Your relationship with the principal supervisor is on the verge of faltering. While you have an imagined identity as a brilliant supervisor and doing your best to support your supervisees, the supervision arrangement is not working out. Rather than joy and excitement, you feel quite distressed and frustrated. Your wellbeing is starting to deteriorate.

While some supervisors get along very well, others have ways of being and doing, including communicating that may not always be in sync with yours. Although everyone on the supervision team is likely to want to support their supervisee, no two supervisors do this in the same way.

Sometimes all you need to do is sit down and explain your differences to come to a happy compromise. Concerns will vary depending on the circumstances.

Difficulties might emerge when principal supervisors think that as an ECR you are inexperienced and believe they need to mentor you. For some principal supervisors, all they want from you in the first few months is to sit back and observe. If you want to increase your presence, meet with the principal supervisor and ask if you can contribute more.

Stresses may emerge because principal supervisors are supervising in ways they have always done and haven't critically analyzed what they are doing. If you have an alternative way of supervising, speak up and ask whether you can give this alternative way of supervising a try in a supervision session on a particular topic (i.e., the literature review, academic writing, etc.). The principal supervisor may be open to learning something new. By running a supervision session designed for a particular task, you also prevent any risk of confusing the research candidate with the change in supervision style. Remember team supervision is a collaboration, not a contest. The only winner or loser is the research candidate.

Another common concern is ways of providing feedback. You read and provide detailed comments on the work, and the principal supervisor skims the candidate's work five minutes before the meeting and gives oral feedback. While they have learned a trick or two as to how to process information quickly and have access to the most recent work in the field, you can still feel that this isn't fair. Before you speak up, while written feedback is necessary at some points in supervision, oral feedback might be the best way forward and you might be putting in more work than you need early in the candidature when ideas are still being formulated. Sometimes they are purposely not giving written feedback to give you a chance to build rapport with the research candidate. You may want to wait before you object. If you find that you are the only supervisor who produces written feedback midway through the candidature, you need to speak up.

A completely different concern is when you have a major role in the supervision, but this is not reflected in your workload allocation. The principal supervisor is rarely around. They go off to conferences and give keynote addresses while you stay home and do most of the supervision. While you and the supervisee reap benefits from co-supervising with a 'famous' researcher, you need to think how much this association is worth to your CV. You may want to suffer through this supervision arrangement to look after this research candidate's wellbeing but decline future opportunities to co-supervise with this principal supervisor.

You could explain the situation to the supervisor. They may be willing to give you some of their workload allocation. Alternatively, you could quietly talk to your Head of School or Department. The famous researcher is probably missing a lot of other departmental activities, so you won't need to explain too much. In your meeting, make sure that you keep your emotions in check as they can be heightened at times like this. There may be ways of topping up your workload allocation.

Most issues with supervision can be resolved through respectful discussion, goodwill, and stepping up and voicing your concerns.

Ultimately, how you deal with the issues will depend on your ways of being and doing, your perseverance, and your resilience. Whatever you do, it's important to maintain a sense of trust. It takes a lot of work to rebuild trust with your colleagues if trust has been compromised, regardless of who is responsible. Whatever you do, don't raise your issues with your principal supervisor in the presence of the research candidate.

Finally, before you put all the blame on others, reflect a little about what you have been doing. As an ECR, being a supervisor is a new way of being. Although you may not want to admit it, the principal supervisor may interrupt you or take over the session because they want to steer you away from problematic ways of doing. Are you voicing opinions about other research candidates, making overly forceful comments, telling the candidate what to do rather than guiding them to do it, or making repeated comments such as 'in my PhD, my supervisors did x'? If the principal supervisor interrupts you, there might be a good reason. You could ask if there are some things you could improve on.

If there is no apparent solution and problems with supervision are keeping you awake at night, making you feel guilty, disappointed, or powerless, you need to act. Withdrawing from the team may be the only option.

Further reading

Clegg and Gower's (2021) blog provides useful statistics on the supervisors' experiences of supervision. Difficulties arise over the lack of clarity in institutions over recognition of workload, and whether supervision time is recognized as research. If you are having some difficulty as a supervisor, you are not alone. Han and Xu (2021) put the emotional aspects of supervision under the spotlight. Their work reinforces the notion that learning to be a supervisor is as much a personal journey as it is about acquiring technical ways of doing.

References

Clegg, Karen, & Gower, Owen. (2021). PhD supervisors need better support, recognition and reward. https://wonkhe.com/blogs/phd-supervisors-need-better-support-recognition-and-reward (accessed 18/1/2024).

Han, Ye, & Xu, Yueting. (2021). Unpacking the emotional dimension of doctoral supervision: Supervisors' emotions and emotion regulation strategies. *Frontiers in Psychology, 12*, 2478–2489, https://doi.org/10.3389/fpsyg.2021.651859

43. Supervising doctoral 'orphans'

Supervision can be a challenge. It can be more so if you take on supervision with a candidate already part way through their doctoral journey.

Before you accept to take on the research candidate, meet with the existing committee members or the person in charge of graduate supervision in your department or school to find out what you can about the research candidate and their thesis topic. If the supervisor you are replacing is no longer at the university, see if you can locate them for a quick chat.

If you feel that you have little to offer the thesis, it's not a good idea to agree to take on a research candidate. Be brave. Explain that you don't feel you have the content or experience necessary to supervise in this situation at this point in your ECR journey. There are more experienced supervisors (perhaps even outside your department or school) who can take this supervision. Your graduate researcher will find someone.

There are other factors to consider before taking on supervision. If the candidate is nearing the end of their candidature, there will be little time for you to get up to speed on their project. With every new supervisor, change is inevitable. If you think there is insufficient time to enable the research candidate to make changes that you will be happy with, say so. In the end, your name will be associated with this thesis.

If you think you can help the doctoral candidate through the rest of their journey, arrange a meeting with the research candidate.

In your meeting take time to find out more about the research candidate's topic. This is the time to raise topics for potential change. You might say that you can supervise under certain conditions. For example, you might want one of the research questions removed or reworked. You might find that the research candidate welcomes the change, or you might find that they are resistant to change in ways that make it impossible for you to work with them.

In your initial exploratory meeting, it's important to find out as much as possible about the research candidate's abilities and interests. The more information you have, the greater your capacity to make an informed decision about whether you are the right person to help this candidate succeed.

If you decide to take on the supervision, talk to the candidate about the need to know about how prior supervision sessions were organized. What was the structure of the supervision meetings, how did the candidate receive feedback? If you would like to do something different, explain your preferences and ask the candidate what they think about these ways of doing it. Your supervisee might be very happy to make changes. If you don't explain changes to their previous ways of doing, this can add confusion to an already delicate situation. There will be times when you should adjust to their previous ways of supervision, where possible. It can give them a perception of continuity.

Finally, if you take on the supervision be vigilant about not asking questions or giving replies that cause the candidate to compare or complain. The candidate needs to move forward, not focus on the past. You also need to be on collegial terms with your colleagues, so it's important not to show sides. Whatever you say in your supervision meeting can (and often will) get back to the previous supervisor.

Further reading

Candidates who have lost supervisors can find it difficult to transition to a new supervisor. Wisker and Robinson (2013) focus on the needs of supervisors and candidates taking up supervision midway through a candidature.

Reference

Wisker, Gina, & Robinson, Gillian. (2013). Doctoral 'orphans': Nurturing and supporting the success of postgraduates who have lost their supervisors. *Higher Education Research & Development, 32*(2), 300–313, https://doi.org/10.1108/17597511311316982

Next steps

Overview

As you prepare to move forward in your career, you have endless possibilities. The first pointer in this chapter focuses on helping you mold your CV for the position you desire and write it in a way that reflects who you are and who you want to be. The next pointer considers how selective choices over sessional employment can build your ways of doing. We then move to coveted research positions, including the post-doc asking if this is something within or outside your reach. We then explore the tricky business of applying for promotion, and how to judge when and why to apply, and what to do if you miss out on your ideal job to help you move forward in your career journey. Final pointers consider how you might explore changes in career direction, and the all-encompassing need to take care of yourself (Figure 9.1).

Figure 9.1 What steps do you want to take?

DOI: 10.4324/9781003481034-9

44. Writing yourself into your CV

For any job application, grant, or book proposal, you need a CV that sells you and your ways of being and doing. Research shows that employers spend on average eight–ten seconds reading a resumé. If there are few candidates or you are applying for a high level position, they may consider your application for a little longer.

With those time restrictions, you need a CV that prioritizes relevant information. For example, a CV for a book proposal is typically very short and focused on publications and not much else; a CV for a grant application contains information about your recent research history and grant success over the last few years. A CV for a teaching position concentrates on teaching, connected administrative roles, and evaluations thereof. If the teaching position includes supervision, this is also included. When applying for a teaching position, publications or grants appear toward the end of your CV, if at all. For a research position, your publications and grants are key to your success. If the position you are applying for counts supervision as a form of research, you include your prior supervision experience. For a position in industry, you give greater prominence to team leadership and administrative roles and rework your teaching skills as expertise in communication.

As you will be applying for different positions with different selection criteria, you need to keep track of all details about your professional development, publications, grant success, teaching, administrative roles, leadership, and supervision in a central location. You can easily lose track of bits: DOIs, dates, and titles of professional training or any theses you supervise. Finding and compiling information for a last minute job application can be a nightmare if you don't have all your information on hand.

To be successful, your CV needs more than the facts. It needs to tie the bits together in a way that paints a picture of who you are and your unique ways of being and doing. This narrative could be in a short paragraph placed before the content of each major section (i.e., teaching experience, publications, etc.) of your CV. This paragraph explains how the documented prior lived experiences in each section of your CV connect, the common threads in your work, and even how experience (i.e., a publication or grant, etc.) builds on another. The titles of your publications and grants don't tell a complete story.

To increase your chances further, you need to draw on another narrative: the organizational narrative where you want to work (i.e., do they emphasize teamwork and leadership; do they value innovation and entrepreneurial approaches?). Organizations like to hire like-minded individuals. Add a sentence or two in your CV, where relevant, to highlight how your lived experiences fit with the culture of the organization where you want to work. This shows interest in the position and that you did not apply simply because the position was available. You may have to dig deep to find some connections, but they will be there. If nothing else, this information shows that you are keen and well-prepared. If there are discontinuities between what you have achieved and the organization's interests explain them. You might explain why your publications are single if there is something in the position description that suggests the panel may have a preference toward co-authored works.

Some CVs end with a very brief section on extra-curricular activities. Volunteer positions can say a lot about you. Coaching local sports teams can be used as supplementary evidence of team building, leadership, or an interest in community outreach. Volunteering in a hospital or healthcare facility shows potential compassion. Outdoor hobbies can give you an edge if you are applying for a job in a rural or remote area. Don't be exhaustive. Reveal the best about yourself, *believe* in yourself, and package your extra-curricular activities to fit. If your extra-curricular activities don't align with your desired position, don't include them.

At the very end of many CVs, you may have a list of three or four potential referees. Sometimes this is a requirement of the application. Even if it's not a requirement, it is a good idea to include them. Think about their references as potential supplementary corroboratory evidence in support of claims in your CV. Current information about you relating to most of the criteria in the job description is essential. It may not be a good idea to list referees from times gone by. They won't do you any favors if they haven't witnessed the accomplishments the organization wants to hear about.

Finally, some ECRs have discontinuous career trajectories. If this is you, it is best to address this in your cover letter. If you took time off to do something else, try to word this in ways that make your experiences count. If you spent time off for childcare, you might write a sentence about what you have learned in that time (i.e., time management, logistics, financial literacy, etc.). These ways of doing can be useful for administrative roles. If possible, ensure any clarifying statements connect to your overall narrative.

If your career trajectory was discontinuous for other reasons (i.e., you received grants in a seemingly unrelated field, or your publications cover topics outside the position description), don't shy away from this. Explain why these are part of your CV and how they give strength to you as an ECR.

If you really want this position, before you submit your application seek feedback from a mentor or colleague who knows you well. They can help you with finetuning wording, suggest lived experiences that you might have forgotten to mention, and point to formatting that might improve the presentation of your CV.

Good Luck!

Further reading

Chong and Clohisey (2021) provide advice on preparing yourself for employment in industry and academia. Their focus is on the modern workplace and how to demonstrate relevant ways of knowing, being, and doing in your CV. This article includes a checklist for CV writing to help you organize information in your CV. Hay (2017) provides advice on preparing academic CVs and cover letters.

References

Chong, Zheng-Shan, & Clohisey, Sara. (2021). How to build a well-rounded CV and get hired after your PhD. *The FEBS Journal, 288*(10), 3072–3081, https://doi.org/10.1111/febs.15635

Hay, Iain. (2017). Write a compelling job application. In *How to be an academic superhero*, pp. 66–71. Edward Elgar. https://doi.org/10.4337/9781786438126.00020

45. Using sessional work to your advantage

You may not have an ideal position to apply for now or can't commit to the rigidity of full time work. Casual employment might be an option for you.

The casual work available will depend on the sector. Most sessional work in academia comes in the form of teaching, marking, or research project support. Industry work may come in the form of administrative work and field experience. Community or government work may involve extensive data analysis. All are valuable to building your ways of knowing and doing. Project work helps build your managerial knowledge. Teaching is great for honing your communication skills. Teaching in subjects related to your research interests shares your ways of knowing, and it helps keep you up-to-date with current reading in the field. Teaching general subjects broadens your experiences and gives you hands-on experience communicating and interacting with large groups.

Marking is perhaps the least enjoyable of all sessional work, and the one least useful for your CV, although it can have short and long term uses. It pays well and gives you the freedom to work outside set hours and work to your own schedule. You can break up the marking with a midday run. If you have health or family concerns, this might be useful short term work. Although marking is tedious and often solitary, it does create opportunities to see the wealth of student diversity first hand. Some students write in ways that are a pure joy to read, some don't get everything right or even understand basic principles. Responding to written work helps to finetune your ways of communicating. It requires practice to stay positive. It also gives you insights into good and bad forms of assessment that help you when you design your own course or apply for a full time position and are asked if you have any experience with curriculum.

Sessional work of all kinds has advantages. It can build contacts with researchers and teaching staff who know about future work opportunities. If you have secured one sessional position, it is often easier to get another.

Sessional work gives you inside information about being part of the wider organization, its work culture, and if this is where you want ongoing work. If you are well-treated and respected as a casual employee, you are likely to be respected in other forms of employment in that workplace.

It is important not to get too cozy in any casual job. While it is easy to do the same task year after year, it doesn't add much to your lived experiences. It helps, if possible, to look for sessional work at several institutions. Taking on a diversity of positions quickly builds your CV. Even if it is the same job you do in two organizations, it builds your CV, by giving you access to different types of learning environments, policies, and curricula. It also positions you to compare work environments. Working as a casual in more than one organization grows your work connections. The more connections, the more opportunities for co-authors, research collaborators, mentors, or referees for your next job application.

Casual work in an organization means that you are a known quantity. This may mean that you have the right to apply for a position as an internal candidate. This can increase your chances of getting a full time position.

While being an insider can sometimes work against you, it can help if you get nervous at interviews or tend to undersell yourself. The panel members will be aware of your strengths and may be more willing to overlook some of your performance at an interview if they already know how great you are.

Casual work has other potential benefits, if you make yourself aware of what is available and use it to your advantage. For example, you can use your institutional email when you apply for a full time position. The flexibility and independence of casual work allow you to work on your own projects, perhaps an article for a journal, an application for a post-doc, or the beginnings of a grant application. Your organization may have a library or database that you can use to help with your endeavors. Your organization may have access to software programs that you can for additional purposes (i.e., access to Word for publications you are writing). You may have access to free professional development that increases your ways of knowing and doing and builds your CV for your ideal position.

Further reading

Richardson, Wardale, and Lord (2019) describe and discuss the pros and cons of sessional academic work. This reading provides insights into the different ways ECRs use casual positions.

Reference

Richardson, Julia; Wardale, Dorothy; & Lord, Linley. (2019). The 'double-edged sword' of a sessional academic career. *Higher Education Research & Development*, *38*(3), 623–637, https://doi.org/10.1080/07294360.2018.1545749

46. Is a post-doc for you?

In the search for your ideal position, you might be considering applying for a post-doc. If you want a career in research, a post-doc elevates your status as a researcher and is a great addition to your CV. However, a post-doc isn't for every ECR. To secure a post-doc, you need to have been research active during your doctoral candidature through a thesis by publication or other forms of publication and have that work published in good journals. In other words, you need a CV that other ECRs would envy. You don't have a lot of time to apply post-thesis. Post-docs have limited eligibility. You must have recently completed your doctorate.

If you have the credentials and your thesis completion falls within the stipulated time limits, different kinds of opportunities are available. Post-docs can be university, government, or industry funded. Some allow you to pursue your own research agenda in ways that add directly to your established research plan. You can enjoy indulging in your research passion with an income. To succeed in your application, you must have a well-developed project that generally fits with the institution's agenda. You also need a strong argument as to the project's outcomes. A likely outcome may be a book publication and a collection of high impact journal articles.

A second type of post-doc may be advertised as a research associate position. With this post-doc type, you work on someone else's project and have less independence around your work. These post-docs are often funded by successful grants with a lead researcher, with an established research agenda. Your success in obtaining one of these post-docs is based on your specific knowledge. Your thesis topic might be directly related to the post-doc topic, or your thesis (and any publications) have the theoretical or methodological strengths required for the position.

Research associate post-docs build your research profile while you work as part of a team. If your application is successful, enquire about outcomes, and how any co-authorship is decided. Do the answers fit into your long term research plan? Are you free to publish work out of data you were responsible for collecting, and can you continue to do so after the post-doc has concluded?

Before applying for either type of post-doc, check the application to make sure that it is what you want. Although both types of post-doc positions can be pure research, some limited teaching or supervision may be attached to the position.

Both types of post-doc are short term stepping stones, providing you with research training and time for research outputs that can set you up for a tenured research position. If you are pumping out publications, successive post-doc positions might be possible. Sometimes the lead researcher has a history of grant applications and intends to apply for follow-up grants that might help keep you employed but it won't be long term. You will need a large grant (see Chapter 6 for details) or be on the lookout for full time employment.

If the prospect of a post-doc looks appealing, check your networks regularly for advertisements, as some applications are advertised in a limited way. Being in the loop is vital.

Further reading

The opportunity to pursue research passions through post-docs can be both exciting and useful, but it pays to be careful. Herschberg, Benschop, and Van Der Brink (2018) consider three constraints around post-doc positions: control over projects, contracts, and potential career trajectories. This is an important reading if you are undecided whether the post-doc is for you. Koens, Hessels, Vogelezang and Vennekens (2024) provides a startling insight into the precarious nature of post-doc and other ECR career paths.

References

Herschberg, Channah; Benschop, Yvonne; & Van den Brink, Marieke. (2018). Precarious postdocs: A comparative study on recruitment and selection of early-career researchers. *Scandinavian Journal of Management, 34*(4), 303–310, https://doi.org/10.1016/j.scaman.2018.10.001

Koens, Lionne; Hessels, Laurens; Vogelezang, Suzanne; & Vennekens, Alexandra. (2024). *An insecure start – Early-career researchers on the barriers they experience*. Den Haag.

47. Building resilience: missing out and nailing it next time

While research credentials and a well-written CV that sells you and your research help secure a job, most ECRs apply for more than one position before they are successful. Although it is cold comfort to know that everyone misses out on dream jobs, it's important to apply every chance you get. You won't get the position if you don't apply.

If your applications are being knocked back, there are a few things you can do. Go back to your CV and find ways to improve your narrative (see Pointer 44 on crafting a CV). Look for any gaps, pick up sessional work to build your lived experiences and expand your ways of being and doing for when the next ideal position is advertised. If you want a research position, start new work and list it in your CV as a manuscript in progress.

If you are shortlisted, well done! Congratulate yourself. You have aced your CV. The selection panel believes you have the necessary lived experiences to undertake the job, your CV has piqued their interest, and you have placed yourself ahead of others.

Another hurdle is your reference check. If you are being shortlisted but not getting an interview, perhaps you need to rethink how you liaise with your referees about any job applications. Whatever you do, notify all potential referees before you apply, send them your CV and the job advertisement, and keep them informed about potential dates for shortlisting so they have ample time to write you a great letter of support.

Think about what your referees write about you. Can they write about current experiences? When you contact your referees, write them a brief note outlining why you would like them to give you a reference. Write different notes to all your potential referees so they highlight different aspects of your knowing, being, doing, and communicating. You don't want referees repeating the same kinds of information. If you get a message back from a potential referee saying they don't feel they would be the best person to give you a reference, don't plead with them. If the only first-hand information they have about you is dated, or not relevant to your application, they won't be able to write you a good reference.

If you think one of your referees might be letting you down, ask if they are willing to share their letter with you. You might consider changing your referees if they don't want to share.

The interview can be another stumbling block. If you got this far, congratulate yourself! The panel has decided that you are one of the best candidates for this job.

There are many reasons why you may not get past the interview, and some of them do not have anything to do with you. In the interview, your job is to convince the panel that your future research plans, career directions, and your ways of being, doing, and communicating align with their expectations of the person they want for this position. Matching what the panel has in mind for the position increases your chances of success, but it doesn't guarantee it. A better match may be waiting for their interview.

Sometimes, however, you might be able to do more.

When the chair introduces the panel, listen carefully to the names of the panel members, perhaps write them down and ask for clarification if you think you didn't hear them correctly. Most people like it when you address them by name. Being able to address panel members by name demonstrates respect and shows that you pay attention to detail.

After you have introduced yourself and your research, panel members often ask questions about how you see your fit in a program or the organization. This question helps them judge how well you have prepared for the interview. It is important to do prior research and have the names of researchers, programs, and research institutes clear in your mind.

Another likely question asked toward the end of the interview is: do you have anything you would like to ask? Asking questions sends positive signals to the panel that you are excited about taking up this position. It's also an opportunity to find out if there are any aspects of the position that you do not appeal to you (i.e., heavy teaching, irregular working hours, excessive expectations on publication, and grant success).

If all of the above are things you do regularly in interview contexts, it is time to consider how you present yourself in stressful contexts. Do you seek clarification on questions you don't quite understand? Missing the point of a question or waffling does nothing for you. The panel is more than willing to repeat or rephrase a question.

Perhaps the length of your answers is causing trouble. Perhaps you ramble or provide too little detail. If most of your answers are shorter than four or five sentences, you may not be explaining yourself in enough detail. If much longer, the panel doesn't have a lot of time to ask you important questions. Instead of stating everything you know, offer a couple of ideas to the panel that you can elaborate on, and offer to give further details if interested. A good interview keeps the flow of interaction between you and the panel members. When they can ask more questions, they get a better idea of who you are and how you like to work. Most ECRs are nervous in interview contexts. Perhaps your nerves are getting the better of you. When nervous, do you have difficulty getting your thoughts together? Do you speak so softly or speak in a way that makes you appear unsure? Such behaviors suggest to the interview panel that you lack self-confidence. There are ways to help. Practicing interview answers can help you look and feel more confident, and help you develop productive ways of framing replies to questions.

Recording yourself in a mock interview and discussing the video with friends helps pick up subtle verbal and non-verbal cues that might not be working in your favor. For example, sometimes when you are nervous, you might forget to smile or greet people when they are first introduced to you! Or perhaps you don't make regular eye contact when you are asked a question.

Maybe you thought you did everything well but still missed out. As mentioned earlier, someone else who was interviewed for the position may have been a better fit. You can't do anything about your competition except to be assured that if your competitor got the job you wanted, they are less likely to compete with you for your next position.

Contact the panel spokesperson to find out a little more about why you were unsuccessful. A phone call may be better than an email. It's a good idea to be brief and to the point and show a positive mindset in the discussion. There might be another opportunity coming up there soon.

Further reading

Naim et al.'s (2015) conference paper underlines the importance of what you say, how you say it, and non-verbal behaviors that you might want to avoid in interviews.

Reference

Naim, Iftekhar; Tanveer, M. Iftekhar; Gildea, Daniel; & Hoque, Mohammed (Ehsan). (2015, May). Automated prediction and analysis of job interview performance: The role of what you say and how you say it. In *2015 11th IEEE International Conference and Workshops on Automatic Face and Gesture Recognition (FG)* (Vol. 1, pp. 1–6). https://www.cs.rochester.edu/~gildea/pubs/naim-fg15.pdf

48. Promotion

You have a great job, and you want to apply for promotion. You feel your achievements are worthy, you want access to new opportunities to further your career.

While some of you may need to apply for promotion as part of the tenure process, other ECRs have more choice when or if to apply. Regardless, to be successful you need to self-promote. Self-promotion makes many ECRs feel uncomfortable. It is challenging and for many ECRs filled with trepidation and self-doubt.

Sometimes this doubt is realistic. Before you work on a promotion application, ask for advice about whether you are career ready. It can be challenging to make this assessment on your own and devastating if you put in a premature application. To circumvent this eventuality, ask your manager or head of department what they think about your potential success. In some organizations, your head is instructed to tell everyone to apply. Ask if that is the case, and if so, turn the question around. 'If you had this CV, would you apply for promotion this year? If not, what would you do to improve your chances if you applied in a year or two?' Be open to critical feedback. While you could still proceed with your application, it is often better to wait, add to your qualifications and experience, and apply later.

If you have the approval of leadership to move forward, you need to craft your application. This takes time and a lot of work. You need all your details and documents lined up well before you apply. If you are thinking about applying for a promotion in a year or two, finetune your CV now (and keep it updated). Reflect back on Pointer 44 for constructing your CV.

A promotion application involves documentation of what you have achieved and an explanation of how these achievements demonstrate why you should be promoted. This narrative needs to be clear, concise, and believable. Your narrative needs to be clear so that those on the committee who are outside your field understand your work and its importance. It needs to be concise so the committee can focus on the main points and not get lost in the details. To be believable, it needs to be easily verified through your CV. This narrative cannot be rushed and will require multiple drafts.

Be brave and pass the narrative for your promotion application around to your mentor, friends, and close colleagues. If they don't understand and believe in your text you need to rewrite, and develop the resolve to rewrite again, if necessary. Listen carefully to any suggestions throughout the process. Believe in yourself, or you won't be believable to others.

Once you have a draft you are happy with, ask someone in leadership to look over the application. This involves completing the application in ample time to embed their feedback into your narrative. Your managers and head of school know what the panel will think, as they have been on many promotion panels during their careers. They can help with wording if you ask for assistance. Being reluctant to ask for help is your worst enemy.

Once the application is complete and submitted, there are two possible outcomes. If successful, you can celebrate your success and create another research plan that states when you want your next promotion and what you plan to do to get it. It never hurts to plan early.

If you weren't successful, ask why. Perhaps make an appointment with the chair of the panel. Listen carefully to what they say and ask what you can do to work toward promotion in a year or two. Resilience is the key. Many researchers stop applying once they are turned down for promotion. This will achieve nothing for your career. Success is not easy.

If your application(s) continue to be unsuccessful and you think your work is deserving, now might be the time to apply for a position outside your institution. Applying for positions at other institutions can accelerate your career if you are ready and able to move. If you get an offer from another institution but unsure if you would like to move, you can go back to your institution with your offer and ask if they can match it. Do this only if you have a firm offer (in writing) and are willing to move.

Further reading

Bosquet, Combes, and García-Peñalosa (2019) report the outcomes of academic promotions in France. They found that the greatest impediment when female academics apply for promotion is the tendency to self-censor their sense of worth. De Paola, Ponzo, and Scoppa (2017) point to a second issue. They found that women in the Italian context were less likely to apply for promotion than men. They hypothesized that the reasons for this were related to ways of being that avoid risk-taking. They also pointed to a lack of self-confidence and even a fear of gender discrimination. In fields where female leadership is low; these factors occur more often.

The advice in both of these articles applies to anyone, regardless of gender, age, ability, or ethnicity.

References

Bosquet, Clément; Combes, Pierre-Philippe; & García-Peñalosa, Cecilia. (2019). Gender and promotions: Evidence from academic economists in France. *The Scandinavian Journal of Economics, 121*(3), 1020–1053, https://doi.org/10.1111/sjoe.12300

De Paola, Maria; Ponzo, Michela; & Scoppa, Vincenzo. (2017). Gender differences in the propensity to apply for promotion: Evidence from the Italian scientific qualification. *Oxford Economic Papers, 69*(4), 986–1009, https://doi.org/10.1093/oep/gpx023

49. Changing career direction

Circumstances change. Workplace restructuring has become relatively commonplace. With restructuring your job can vanish or change in ways you can't accept, and you have no choice but to look for other employment. In other situations, your job is secure but family needs mean a change in employment. Your partner may be offered a position in another city, and you want to support their choice, or you may have unexpected caregiving that makes the combination of your current job and these added responsibilities impossible to manage. Perhaps it is the job itself that is causing a need for change. If your current job makes you feel constantly exhausted or is not sufficiently challenging and you are bored out of your mind, it's time for a career change.

For some of you, the prospect of change fills your heart with joy. You relish change and enjoy the thought of leaping from one academic setting to the next or from academia to industry to government and see it as an important strategy to turbocharge your career. You do not intend to stay in any job and see each position as a stepping stone to build your ways of knowing, being, doing, and communicating to make the next step happen.

For some of you though, the prospect of change is terrifying. You may be someone who only contemplates changing your career direction when the alternative of staying where you are is no longer tenable (for any of the reasons listed above). If you find change daunting, you might like to consider small changes. Perhaps you would love different conditions: different hours, a steadier income; limited or no after-hours work; better promotion opportunities but haven't ever asked about this. Be brave and schedule time to talk to your manager about ways that you think would make your life and your job more manageable and more enjoyable. To structure your discussion, it helps to be prepared. Some of the information in our pointer on interview techniques (Pointer 47) might help. If there is no support from your manager for such a small change, you are probably not in a position where you are valued. Gain courage and apply for a position in another department in the same organization. That way you won't need to move, and you will still have friends and colleagues around to support you.

Bigger shifts are sometimes needed. These might involve changing sectors: from academia to industry, or government, or community positions. Changing sectors requires building your CV in different ways (see Pointer 44). Each sector values different ways of conducting research, different kinds of knowledge, different ways of doing, and different ways of writing and oral communication. To move into another sector, you need to repackage your ways of knowing and doing, and rework and reword them. For example, grant success is prized in universities and the community sector and in government, but not for the same reasons. Universities and the community sector value the funds, the university sector also values the prestige. In a government position, your grant success is prized, but differently. Here it demonstrates the ability to write convincingly, and critique grants written by others. Depending on your grant, your lived experience as a successful grant holder can be used to show a willingness toward community outreach.

To understand how your existing ways of being, doing, knowing, and communicating can be transferred to your target sector, it is best to draw on inside knowledge. You may know someone who could mentor you on how to restructure and relabel your CV (see Pointer 8 on mentors). Career counselors can be very helpful in working out what you need for the position, what you already know, and how you can reframe those ways of knowing for the target sector. Both mentors and counselors can also advise on gaps in your ways of knowing and doing, and how you might gain lived experiences to help fill those gaps. You may need professional development if you have gaps in your IT skills. A certificate in policy development, leadership, or management is a great addition to your CV if you want to shift into a government position. A teaching certificate is often necessary if you want a job in the school system. You can do many certificates online these days. If you need a job in academia, you might try to publish a short article before you apply. If you decide to publish an article, revisit your publication plan (Pointer 12), look closely at anything you have published, and see if something might be reworked for an outlet more suited to your desired sector.

Another place to visit is your social media strategy (Pointer 3). Are you in the right network? Are there networks used by those from your target sector that you could join? Get help from someone in the sector. They know where you should look. When you sign up you will need to put up your social profile. Have an insider look into it before you post it online. You don't want to sound like an outsider.

If you want to get into a position from another sector, you might also consider whether there is part time work (Pointer 45). In academia, you might take a part time position as a tutor or take on some marking. If you are in government or industry and you want to shift to academia, you might make inquiries about supporting a research student. This might work well if you work if your current position is receptive to taking interns.

Keep trying until you get shortlisted. If you persist with your goals and are lucky enough to convince an interview panel that you will fit very nicely in their organization, you are well on your way to your new career (see Pointer 47 on resilience).

An alternative approach is to set up your own consultancy business. You might like to work with NGOs, or run an editing business. Owning your own business means you won't need to suffer through interviews, but you will need to promote yourself extensively through social media and draw on other contacts you have.

Consultancies take time to establish, and you may need to look for casual or part-time work to tide you over at the beginning. Working on your own can be challenging, but it can also be very rewarding.

Changing sectors is not easy, and you may need to persist before you finally get where you want. Few people now expect to remain in any job for their lifetime. Career change has become the new norm.

Further reading

Ta et al. (2024) recount ECR stories of movement in and out of industry, government, and universities in their search for career progression and sustainable employment. If you are considering different pathways, this is a heartening read. Wrosch et al. (2007) focus on redirecting career energies toward more achievable goals and better health.

References

Ta, Binh; Hoang, Cuong; Khong, Hang; & Dang, Trang. (2024). Australian PhD graduates' agency in navigating their career pathways: Stories from social sciences. *Higher Education, 88*, 1525–1545, https://doi.org/10.1007/s10734-024-01181-6

Wrosch, Carsten; Miller, Gregory. E.; Scheier, Michael F.; & De Pontet, Stephanie Brun. (2007). Giving up on unattainable goals: Benefits for health? *Personality and Social Psychology Bulletin, 33*(2), 251–265, https://doi.org/10.1177/0146167206294905

50. Taking care of yourself

This might be the last pointer in this book, but it is by no means an afterthought. Concepts and strategies of selfcare underlie all pointers and are implicit in our thinking about all aspects of ECR life and how no ECR is the same.

Your life history is unique, and your desires and how you imagine yourself and your ECR career differ from other ECRs. This affects how you experience and interpret your world, the goals you set for yourself, and how your research impacts on your ways of being, doing, and communicating. If you are feeling happy and healthy, you can achieve far more for yourself and others. Trying to be all things to everyone is exhausting. Being constantly exhausted will achieve very little for anyone.

Selfcare is so important. Many things demand your attention: work, your community, your family, and friends. It is critical to find ways to care for yourself and prioritize those things that nourish your spirit. You need ways to recharge your batteries so that you have the clarity of thought to put your publications, grants, teaching, management, and supervision into perspective.

It is worth repeating to ourselves ways to keep healthy. Take brief moments for yourself. Think about a small pleasure that makes you happy and carve time to make it happen. Remember this small pleasure so that it can make you smile for even a moment during the chaos of a working day. Smile whenever you can as smiling is often reciprocal, and a smile in return can make you feel refreshed. Positive comments and gratitude also help. Try to start and end meetings with a positive comment. If you do this often enough you will get positive comments in return.

Pacing yourself can make a difference. Take a few minutes to remember to slow down. Perhaps walk slowly to at least one meeting. Or look out the window for a minute to take in something peaceful from your surroundings.

Stop and think about where you are. Can you work for an hour in the park; a café; a library; or the back of a bookstore where you can work undisturbed? Can you work at home, perhaps curled up on the couch with a laptop and a coffee? Could you change something in your home or workspace to make your time more productive? In addition to having your computer, desk, and chair to suit your physical needs, do you have a comfortable chair you can rest in to reflect and think or ponder over spreadsheets?

Time is finite and we all need ways to achieve some balance. The traditional workday allowed eight hours to work, eight hours for leisure, and eight hours for sleep. Technology has blurred these boundaries. You now need to set your own boundaries.

If you can't find time in your working day, think about waking up a little earlier. You might start your day with something you have been putting off because you feel there is no time. Perhaps a ½ hour for research or grant writing before you go to work or a ½ hour before you go home. You might do this for a short time, but you still need balance.

Perhaps you can organize your existing day to make life better. Or you could set times to respond to emails or specific times of the day for meetings, so they don't constantly interrupt your train of thought. Avoid interruptions where possible. Turn off the button on your computer that says you have received an email or the beeping sound on your phone that alerts you to an incoming message. If you are constantly being interrupted, think about putting up a sign to make time to gather your thoughts (Figure 9.2).

Have a play with the wording of your sign to make it more you. You might prefer to designate times such as: Between 9 and 10 is my "me time" so I

My door is usually open. Please **do not knock if its closed.**

If I am in the office, I am

- In a private meeting
- Trying to do something very important.
- Email me, or slip a note under my door, or come back at the hours listed on my door. I will be very happy to talk to you then.

Figure 9.2 What sign do you have on your door?

can think about what I have to do for the day. Or if research time is frustrating you: I have been trying to work on a publication (or grant) but finding I don't have time. I have allocated 9–10 am every morning to help further my thinking. Please respect my limited time and come back later.

This permanent sign will help others respect your needs and keep you to your promise. You don't want to be seen responding to an email or going for a coffee during the times you have designated on your door.

Think carefully about your commitments. Try to avoid anything that disrupts your research plans. Setting priorities and declining offers is easier if you have research plans that support your goals.

Personal time is a necessity. This does not necessarily mean going off to yoga and meditation classes (but if this is you, go for it). For many, it might be cooking, watching reality TV, reading a romance novel or a spy thriller, gardening, or walking through the bushland, on the beach, or in a park. There are great benefits in just spending some time alone and letting your thoughts unwind. You can afford an hour a day for you.

You can also afford a night or two off to socialize with your family, friends, and community. Things that help take your mind away from work, such as date nights with your partner, girls'/boys' nights out (or in), or simply watching a football, hockey, or cricket game or catching up on the gossip are important. Family gatherings for a big Sunday lunch or BBQ are great for selfcare. Your connections help make your work matter; as others who are important to you will better understand your contribution. It allows them to show their care for you.

Staying healthy can also mean doing nothing. Good sleep routines help thought. You might not get eight hours (Lucky you if you can!) but you should plan for sleep. Add an hour of winding down time before your head hits the pillow. Keep a notepad handy for when the winding down generates great ideas so that you avoid the temptation to reach for your phone or laptop. Bright lights on electronic gadgets keep you awake. If you like to nap, a short powernap can give the brain a little extra rest. There is no excuse for not taking a powernap when you work from home.

Maintaining balance is the key to good physical and emotional health. Find ways to center yourself if (when) you feel out of balance. And talk. Family or community members can be good listeners. It's important not to keep everything bottled up inside. Setting up positive forms of work-life balance strategies early in your career will set the stage for the rest of your career.

Further reading

We recommend two chapters in *Women practicing resilience, self-care and wellbeing in academia*. Sum's chapter (2023) is an inspiring narrative of her transition to an ECR during the COVID-19 pandemic. She reflects on her creation of a safe place, and the importance of solitude to allow herself to unravel the bewildering experience of being and doing as an ECR. Sum drew on a network of 'pseudo-mentors' (or in our terms, peers and other informal mentors) to support her identity transition and provide her with role models to 'refuel' her passion. Randa (2023) includes an interesting discussion on mindfulness and ways women in leadership have used this to build their resilience. Nicol and Yee's (2017) autoethnographic account gives insight into personal priorities and professional decision making. They describe 'self-care' through personal and professional ways of knowing, being, and doing. They include personal and professional ways of feeling into their selfcare.

References

Nicol, Donna J., & Yee, Jennifer A. (2017). "Reclaiming our time": Women of color, faculty and radical self-care in the academy. *Feminist Teacher, 27*(2–3), 133–156.

Randa, Moreoagae Bertha. (2023). Of wellbeing and self-care in academia. In Lemon (Ed.), *Women practicing resilience, self-care and wellbeing in academia*. pp. 186–198. Routledge. https://doi.org/10.4324/9781003341482-18

Sum, Nicola. (2023). Solitude, sanctuary, and pseudo-mentors: A pandemic lens on an early career transition into doing and being research/researcher. In Lemon (Ed.), *Women practicing resilience, self-care and wellbeing in academia,* pp. 57–68. Routledge. https://doi.org/10.4324/9781003341482-18

Afterword: using Artificial Intelligence (AI) in research

When the reviewers of this book commented on our book proposal, one request was to consider the role of AI in Early Career research. We pondered this idea and largely dismissed it as something that we knew little about. Discussions with our children who knew more about the subject than us proved helpful.[1] They suggested we ask AI, and with their assistance, we posed a question to ChatGPT (Version 4).

The initial question posed was: How can AI assist early career research?

We provided parameters of 300–400 words and asked for the text to be written in a lively and engaging style. The following is ChatGPT's response to our question.

> *AI can be a game-changer for early-career researchers, helping them work smarter, faster, and more efficiently. Whether you're struggling with literature reviews, data analysis, or even writing, AI has tools that can make the research process smoother and less overwhelming.*
>
> *1. Finding and Synthesizing Research*
>   *One of the biggest challenges for new researchers is keeping up with the ever-growing mountain of academic papers. AI-powered tools like Elicit, Semantic Scholar, and ResearchRabbit can help by summarizing papers, highlighting key findings, and even suggesting relevant studies you might have missed. Instead of spending hours sifting through PDFs, AI can help you focus on the most relevant research.*
> *2. Writing and Editing Assistance*
>   *Writing is a crucial part of research, but it can be daunting. AI-driven writing assistants like Grammarly, ChatGPT, and QuillBot*

Afterword: using Artificial Intelligence (AI) in research

can help refine your prose, check for clarity, and even suggest alternative phrasing. If English isn't your first language, AI translation tools like DeepL can make your writing more polished and professional.

3. Data Analysis and Visualization

Crunching numbers and making sense of complex datasets is another area where AI shines. Platforms like MATLAB, Python libraries (such as SciPy and TensorFlow), and AI-powered statistical tools like IBM, SPSS, or JASP can help with data processing, pattern recognition, and visualization. This means you can spend less time wrestling with statistics and more time interpreting results.

4. Generating Ideas and Overcoming Writer's Block

Sometimes, the hardest part of research is getting started. AI can act as a brainstorming partner, suggesting research questions, hypotheses, or even outlining sections of a paper. While AI won't replace critical thinking, it can provide inspiration when you're stuck.

5. Managing Workflows and Productivity

AI can also streamline research workflows. Citation managers like Zotero and EndNote use AI to format references correctly, while project management tools like Notion and Trello can help you stay organized. AI-powered scheduling assistants can even help plan your workload, keeping you on track for deadlines.

The Bottom Line

AI won't replace human intuition, creativity, or critical thinking, but it can be a powerful assistant for early-career researchers. By automating tedious tasks, improving efficiency, and offering insights, AI allows researchers to focus on what truly matters – making discoveries and advancing knowledge.

ChatGPT.com (V. 4. accessed 03.02.2025)

We had an answer back in minutes. It is certainly a quick way of creating content. Although the response contains lots of details about the broad uses of AI and presents a range of programs that are available and their functions, there was nothing in the AI-generated text to help researchers decide which of the available options listed in the text ChatGPT might suit them better.

Afterword: using Artificial Intelligence (AI) in research

We were also struck by the impersonal tone of the writing. We had asked for the text to be 'lively and engaging'. In this respect, we think that ChatGPT did not excel. While numbering ideas in a text creates clarity, it doesn't equate to lively and engaging text. We also felt that the English read as formulaic, the kind of academic English that provides information about content but not about the speaker/writer of the text. In some respects, it is the kind of antithesis to our position where we ask thesis writers and ECRs to write in ways that build on their lived experiences, ways of being, doing, and communicating to make their text their own.

We thought that perhaps our result might have had something to do with the sources ChatGPT used to respond to our question, so we asked an additional question.

What sources does ChatGPT draw on to provide advice for Early Career Researchers to select AI to assist their research? (parameters, 100 words).

The following was its response.

ChatGPT draws on a range of sources including published literature, academic journals, best practices from established research institutions, contributions from peer-reviewed conferences, and historical training data which includes a wide variety of content available publicly. It uses open research data and guidelines available through resources such as arXiv, government reports, and professional organizations' websites. Additionally, its training includes data from books, reputable news sources, and online encyclopedias. Although ChatGPT is not connected to real-time databases, it synthesizes this diverse training content to provide balanced and well-informed advice to researchers. These comprehensive, multi-faceted resources empower nuanced, informed guidance for emerging scholars.

ChatGPT.com (V.4. accessed 11.02.2025).

Reading through this list, we began to ponder another issue, source validity. While you can get quick content by asking questions of AI, publicly available sources are not necessarily reliable sources, and 'reputable' may mean many things. Online encyclopedias often have content that has not been thoroughly fact-checked. These days, the world is flooded with mis- and disinformation and needs to be approached with a certain degree of caution.

We also pondered the wording of our questions; perhaps our first question may not have been framed appropriately. If we asked 'Could ChatGPT write a response as if we phrased it: How could AI help a young female ECR who wants to sound lively and engaging in her conference abstract?' While we might get a better-suited text than the one produced from texts that draw on 'historical training' data, it still might not be text written in ways that adhere to how a particular young female ECR would like to communicate. If mass-produced it might even create additional issues. It runs the risk of producing and reproducing stereotypes. We are also not sure how any person co-authoring with ChatGPT or other programs avoids plagiarism.

However, as we said at the beginning of this pointer, we are not experts on what AI can do for ECRs and even if we were, with so much happening so quickly in this space, it is difficult to offer much advice. Next week our same query might offer suggestions that serve the requested content in ways that are closer to the ECRs own language wants and needs. This kind of AI-generated text might need to draw on prior texts written by the ECR, as well as texts of their friends and colleagues who they interact with online. It might also be changed with a little extra nuancing from whatever else AI has to offer. The privacy issues involved are daunting.

For now, we suggest that you continue working on your own manuscripts and grants and craft them to make them your own. Your text may not always have all the content that AI can generate, but you can feel like you are behind what and how your text is written.

Note

1 The cost of subscriptions to these various tools was not mentioned as an issue. If you are fortunate, your institution might provide this, but as an individual, subscriptions can add up to big money quite quickly.

References

Ahmed, Sarah. J., & Güss, C. Dominik. (2022). An analysis of writer's block: Causes and solutions. *Creativity Research Journal*, *34*(3), 339–354, https://doi.org/10.1080/10400419.2022.2031436

Aiello, Emilia; Donovan, Clair; Duque, Elena; Fabrizio, Serena et al., (2021). Effective strategies that enhance the social impact of social sciences and humanities research. *Evidence & Policy*, *17*(1), 131–146, https://doi.org/10.1332/174426420X15834126054137

Ajebon, Mildred Oiza; Kwong, Yim Ming Connie, & Astorga de Ita, Diego. (2021). *Navigating the field: Postgraduate experiences in social research*. Springer Nature. https://doi.org/10.1007/978-3-030-68113-5

Allen, Jan E., & Chris M. Golde. (2018). *The productive graduate student writer: How to manage your time, process, and energy to write your research proposal, thesis, and dissertation and get published*. Routledge.

Baccarella, Christian V.; Wagner, Timm F.; Kietzman, Jan H., & McCarthy, Ian P. (2018). Understanding the dark side of social media. *European Management Journal*, *36*(4), 431–438, https://doi.org/10.1016/j.emj.2018.07.002

Bataille, Gretchen M., & Brown, Betsy E. (2006). *Faculty career paths: Multiple routes to academic success and satisfaction*. Rowman and Littlefield.

Becker, Lucinda. (2014). *Presenting your research: Conferences, symposiums, poster presentations and beyond*. Sage.

Bentley, Sarah V.; Peters, Kim; Haslam, S. Alexander, & Greenaway, Katherine H. (2019). Construction at work: Multiple identities scaffold professional identity development in academia. *Frontiers in Psychology, 10*(628), 1–10, https://doi.org/10.3389/fpsyg.2019.00628

Borkowski, John G., & Howard, Kimberly S. (2006). Applying for research grants. In Fredrick T. L. Leong & James T. Austin (Eds.), *The psychology research handbook: A guide for graduate students and research assistants*. (2nd ed.), pp. 433–442. Sage.

Bosquet, Clément; Combes, Pierre-Philippe, & García-Peñalosa, Cecilia. (2019). Gender and promotions: Evidence from academic economists in France. *The Scandinavian Journal of Economics*, *121*(3), 1020–1053, https://doi.org/10.1111/sjoe.12300

References

Boynton, Petra. (2020). *Being well in academia: Ways to feel stronger, safer and more connected.* Routledge. https://doi.org/10.4324/9780429197512

Bozeman, Barry, & Youtie, Jan. (2016). Trouble in paradise: Problems in academic research co-authoring. *Science and Engineering Ethics, 22,* 1717–1743, https://doi.org/10.1007/s11948-015-9722-5

Brezis, Elise S., & Birukou, Aliaksandr. (2020). Arbitrariness in the peer review process. *Scientometrics, 123*(1), 393–411, https://doi.org/10.1007/s11192-020-03348-1

Browning, Beverly. A. (2022). *Grant writing for dummies.* (7th ed.) John Wiley & Sons.

Browning, Lynette; Thompson, Kirrilly, & Dawson, Drew. (2017). From early career researcher to research leader: Survival of the fittest? *Journal of Higher Education and Policy Management, 39*(4), 361–377, https://doi.org/10.1080/1360080X.2017.1330814

Burford, James, & Henderson, Emily F. (2023). *Making sense of academic conferences: Presenting, participating and organising.* Routledge. https://doi.org/10.4324/9781003144885

Caffarella, Rosemary S., & Barnett, Bruce G. (2000). Teaching doctoral students to become scholarly writers: The importance of giving and receiving critiques. *Studies in Higher Education, 25*(1), 39–52.

Cantwell, Robert Harley, & Scevak, Jill Janina (Eds.). (2010). *An academic life: A handbook for new academics.* Aust Council for Ed Research.

Cardilini, Adam P.A.; Risely, Alice, & Richardson, Mark F. (2022). Supervising the PhD: Identifying common mismatches in expectations between candidate and supervisor to improve research training outcomes. *Higher Education Research & Development, 41*(3), 613–627, https://doi.org/10.1080/07294360.2021.1874887

Carter, Susan; Guerin, Cally, & Aitchison, Claire. (2020). Managing productivity. In *Doctoral writing: Practices, processes and pleasures,* pp. 51–91. Springer Singapore. https://doi.org/10.1007/978-981-15-1808-9

Chapman, Jacqueline M.; Algera, Dirk; Dick, Melissa; Hawkins, Emily E. et al. (2015). Being relevant: Practical guidance for early career researchers interested in solving conservation problems. *Global Ecology and Conservation, 4,* 334–348, https://dx.doi.org/10.1016/j.gecco.2015.07.013

Chong, Zheng-Shan, & Clohisey, Sara. (2021). How to build a well-rounded CV and get hired after your PhD. *The FEBS Journal, 288*(10), 3072–3081, https://doi.org/10.1111/febs.15635

Clegg, Karen, & Gower, Owen. (2021). PhD supervisors need better support, recognition and reward. https://wonkhe.com/blogs/phd-supervisors-need-better-support-recognition-and-reward (accessed 18/1/2024).

Clews, Simon. (2021). *The new academic: How to write, present and profile your amazing research to the world.* New South Publishing.

Clowes, Lindsay, & Shefer, Tamara (2013). "It's not a simple thing, co publishing": Challenges of co-authorship between supervisors and students in South African higher educational contexts. *Africa Education Review, 10,* 32–47, https://doi.org/10.1080/18146627.2013.786865

References

Costa, Cristina, & Condie, Jenna. (2018). *Doing research in and on the digital: Research methods across fields of enquiry*. Routledge. https://doi.org/10.4324/9781315561622

Crase, Darrell. (1993). Highly productive scholars: What drives them to success? *Journal of Physical Education, Recreation & Dance, 64*(6), 80–82.

Debowski, Shelda. (2012). The *new academic: A strategic handbook*. Open University Press.

Denholm, Carey, & Evans, Terry. (Eds.). (2009). *Beyond doctorates downunder: Maximising the impact of your doctorate from Australia and New Zealand*. (2nd ed.) ACER.

Denicolo, Pam (Ed.). (2013). *Achieving impact in research*. Sage.

Denicolo, Pam, & Reeves, Julie. (2013). *Developing transferable skills: Enhancing your research and employment potential*. Sage.

De Paola, Maria; Ponzo, Michela, & Scoppa, Vincenzo. (2017). Gender differences in the propensity to apply for promotion: Evidence from the Italian scientific qualification. *Oxford Economic Papers, 69*(4), 986–1009, https://doi.org/10.1093/oep/gpx023

Dewan, Pooja, & Gupta, Piyush. (2016). Writing the title, abstract and introduction: Looks matter! *Indian Pediatrics, 53*, 235–241.

Dlaskova, Julie; Mirosa, Romain, & Murachver, Tamar. (2004). Supervisor perceptions of quality postgraduate research candidates. https://www.otago.ac.nz/__data/assets/pdf_file/0024/327471/supervisor-perceptions-of-quality-postgraduate-research-candidates-001461.pdf

Dodgen, Daniel; Fowler, Raymond. D., & Williams-Nickelson, Carol. (2013). Getting involved in professional organizations: A gateway to career advancement. In Mitchell J. Prinstein & Marcus D. Patterson (Eds.), *The portable mentor: Expert guide to a successful career in psychology*, pp. 257–267. Springer https://doi.org/10.1007/978-1-4614-3994-3

Dunleavy, Patrick, & Tinkler, Jane. (2021). *Maximizing the impacts of academic research: How to grow the recognition, influence, practical application and public understanding of science and scholarship*. Macmillan.

Durkin, Mick. (1992). Some dynamics of authorship. *Australia Universities Review, 35*(1), 43–48.

Eley, Adrian. R.; Wellington, Jerry; Pitts, Stephanie, & Biggs, Catherine. (2012). *Becoming a successful early career researcher*. Routledge. https://doi.org/10.4324/9780203113073

Eodice, Michele, & Day, Kami. (2003). *First person squared: A study of co-authoring in the academy*. Utah State University Press. *Project MUSE*. muse.jhu.edu/book/9351

Fenton, Angela; Walsh, Kerryann, & MacDonald, Amy. (2016). Capacity building of early career researchers through cross-institutional mentoring. In B. Gloria Guzman Johannessen (Ed.), *Global co-mentoring networks in higher education: Politics, policies, and practices*, pp. 203–227. Springer. https://doi.org/10.1007/978-3-319-27508-6

References

Folk, Susan, & Pequegnat, Willo. (2011). Common mistakes in proposal writing and how to avoid them. In Willo Pequegnat, Ellen Stover & Cheryl Anne Boyce (Eds.), *How to write a successful grant application: A guide for social and behavioral scientists,* pp. 95–103. Springer. https://doi.org/10.1007/978-1-4419-1454-5_1

Gelman, Sheldon R., & Gibelman, Margaret. (2014). A quest for citations? An analysis of and commentary on the trend toward multiple authorship. *Journal of Social Work Education, 35*(2), 203–213, https://doi.org/10.1080/10437797.1999.10778960

Gerring, John, & Cojocaru, Lee. (2016). Arbitrary limits to scholarly speech: Why (short) word limits should be abolished. *Qualitative & Multi-Method Research, 14,* 2–12, https://doi.org/10.5281/zenodo.823308

Goldsworthy, Jeffrey. (2008). Research grant mania. *The Australian Universities Review, 50*(2), 17–24.

Habibie, Pejman, & Burgess, Sally (Eds.). (2021). *Scholarly publication trajectories of early-career scholars: Insider perspectives.* Palgrave Macmillan. https://doi.org/10.1007/978-3-030-85784-4

Haertling, Amanda Thein, & Beach, Richard. (2010). Mentoring doctoral students towards publication within scholarly communities of practice. In Claire Atchison, Barbara Kamler & Alison Lee (Eds.), *Publishing pedagogies for the doctorate and beyond,* pp. 117–136. Routledge.

Han, Ye, & Xu, Yueting (2021). Unpacking the emotional dimension of doctoral supervision: Supervisors' emotions and emotion regulation strategies. *Frontiers in Psychology, 12,* 2478–2489, https://doi.org/10.3389/fpsyg.2021.651859

Hay, Iain. (2017). *Manage your time: How to be an academic superhero: Establishing and sustaining a successful career in the social sciences and arts and humanities.* Edward Elgar. https://doi.org/10.4337/9781786438126.00025

Hay, Iain. (2017). Write a compelling job application. In *How to be an academic superhero,* pp. 66–71. Edward Elgar. https://doi.org/10.4337/9781786438126.00020

Herschberg, Channah; Benschop, Yvonne, & Van den Brink, Marieke. (2018). Precarious postdocs: A comparative study on recruitment and selection of early-career researchers. *Scandinavian Journal of Management, 34*(4), 303–310, https://doi.org/10.1016/j.scaman.2018.10.001

Huisman, Janine, & Smits, Jeroen. (2017). Duration and quality of the peer review process: The author's perspective. *Scientometrics, 113*(1), 633–650, https://doi.org/10.1007/s11192-017-2310-5

Ismail, Affero; Abiddin, Norhasni Zainal, & Hassan, Aminuddin. (2011). Improving the development of postgraduates' research and supervision. *International Education Studies, 4*(1), 78–89.

Jaeger, Audrey J., & Dinin, Alessandra J. (Eds.). (2018). *The postdoc landscape: The invisible scholars.* Academic Press. https://doi.org/10.1016/B978-0-12-813169-5.02001-2

Janke, Kristin K.; Wilby, Kyle John, & Zavod, Robin. (2020). Academic writing as a journey through "chutes and ladders": How well are you managing your emotions? *Currents in Pharmacy Teaching and Learning, 12*(2), 103–111, https://doi.org/10.1016/j.cptl.2019.11.001

Johnson, Alan M. (2011). *Charting a course for a successful research career: A guide for early career researchers.* (2nd ed.) Elsevier B.V.

Johnson, Suzanne Hall. (1996). Dealing with conflicting reviewers' comments. *Nurse Author & Editor,* 6(4), 1–3.

Kent, Brianne A.; Homan, Constance; Amoako, Emmanuella; Antonietti, Alberto et al. (2022). Recommendations for empowering early career researchers to improve research culture and practice. *PLoS Biol,* 20(7), e3001680, https://doi.org./10.1371/journal.pbio.3001680

Khoo, Tseen; Ward, Phil, & O'Donnell, Jonathan. (2023). *Getting research funded: Five essential rules for early career researchers.* Routledge.

Knight, Linda V., & Steinbach, Theresa A. (2008). Selecting an appropriate publication outlet: A comprehensive model of journal selection criteria for researchers in a broad range of academic disciplines. *International Journal of Doctoral Studies,* 3, 59–79.

Koens, Lionne; Hessels, Laurens; Vogelezang, Suzanne; & Vennekens, Alexandra. (2024). *An insecure start – Early-career researchers on the barriers they experience.* Den Haag.

Koster, Rhonda; Baccar, Kirstine, & Lemelin, R. Harvey. (2012). Moving from research ON, to research WITH and for indigenous communities: A critical reflection on community-based participatory research. *Canadian Geographer, 12,* 195–210, https://doi.org/10.1111/j.1541-0064.2012.00428.x

Koutsantoni, Dimitra. (2009). Persuading sponsors and securing funding: Rhetorical patterns in grant proposals. In Maggie Charles, Diane Pecorari & Susan Hunston (Eds.), *Academic writing: At the interface of corpus and discourse,* pp. 37–57. Continuum International.

Kubach, Douglas; Geiser, Elizabeth; Dolin, Arnold, & Topkis, Gladys. (2019). *The business of book publishing: Papers by practitioners.* Routledge.

Kumar, Smita, & Cavallaro, Liz. (2018). Researcher self-care in emotionally demanding research: A proposed conceptual framework. *Qualitative Health Research,* 28(4), 648–658, https://doi.org/10.1177/1049732317746377

Kumar, Vijay, & Wald, Navé. (2023). Ambiguity and peripherality in doctoral co-supervision workload allocation. *Higher Education Research & Development,* 42(4), 860–873, https://doi.org/10.1080/07294360.2022.2115984

Kwasnicka, Dominika, & Lai, Alden Yuanhong (Eds.). (2022). *Survival guide for early career researchers.* Springer.

Lawes, Mario; Schultz, Martin, & Eid, Michael. (2020). Making the most of your research budget: Efficiency of a three-method measurement design with planned missing data. *Assessment,* 27(5), 903–920, https://doi.org/10.1177/1073191118798050

Lemon, Narelle. (2014). Sending out a tweet: Finding new ways to network in academia. In Narelle Lemon & Suzanne Garvis (Eds.), *Being "In and out": Providing voice to early career women in academia,* pp. 43–54. Springer.

Lemon, Narelle, & Salmons, Janette. (2021). *Reframing and rethinking collaboration in higher education and beyond: A practical guide for doctoral students and early career researchers.* Routledge.

References

Lieff, Susan; Baker, Lindsay; Mori, Brenda; Egan-Lee, Eileen et al. (2012). Who am I? Key influences on the formation of academic identity within a faculty development program. *Medical Teacher, 34*(3), e208–e215, https://doi.org/10.3109/0142159X.2012.642827

Macaulay, Luke. (2023). Entering a career as an ECR in an increasingly shifting academic landscape: The value of different forms of capital. In Basil Cahusac de Caux, Lynette Pretorius & Luke Macaulay (Eds.), *Research and teaching in a pandemic world: The challenges of establishing academic identities during times of crisis*, pp. 327–342. Springer Nature. https://doi.org/10.1007/978-981-19-7757-2

Mahat, Marian, & Tatebe, Jennifer (Eds.). (2019). *Achieving academic promotion*. Emerald. https://doi.org/10.1108/9781787568990

Martin, Annika; Mori, Julia, & Froehlich, Dominik Emanuel. (2023). Career development of Early career researchers via distributed peer mentoring networks. *Merits, 3*, 569–582, https://doi.org/10.3390/merits3030034

Mathioudakis, Alexander G.; Wagner, Darcy, & Bumas, Orianne. (2022). How to peer review: Practical advice for early career researchers. *Breathe, 18*(4), 1–10, https://doi.org/10.1183/20734735.0160-2022

Maunder, Rachel E., (2021). Staff and student experiences of working together on pedagogic research projects: Partnerships in practice. *Higher Education Research & Development, 40*(6), 1205–1219, https://doi.org/10.1080/07294360.2020.1809999

McAlpine, Lynn, & Åkerlind, Gerlese. (2010). *Becoming an academic*. Palgrave Macmillan.

McAlpine, Lynn, & Amundsen, Cheryl. (2018). *Identity-trajectories of early career researchers: Unpacking the post-PhD experience*. Palgrave Macmillan. https://doi.org/10.1057/978-1-349-95287-8

McArdle, Rachel. (2022). Flexible methodologies: A case for approaching research with fluidity. *The Professional Geographer, 74*(4), 620–627, https://doi.org/10.1080/00330124.2021.2023593

McCallum, Carmen. (2017). Giving back to the community: How African Americans envision utilizing their PhD. *The Journal of Negro Education, 86*(2), 138–53, https://doi.org/10.7709/jnegroeducation.86.2.0138

Monereo, Charles, & Liesa, Eva. (2022). Early career researchers' identity positions based on research experiences. *Higher Education Research and Development, 41*(1), 193–210, https://doi.org/10.1080/07294360.2020.1835834

Murgia, Annalisa, & Poggio, Barbara. (Eds.). (2019). *Gender and precarious research careers: A comparative analysis*. Routledge. https://doi.org/10.4324/9781315201245

Naim, Iftekhar; Tanveer, M. Iftekhar; Gildea, Daniel, & Hoque, Mohammed (Ehsan). (2015, May). Automated prediction and analysis of job interview performance: The role of what you say and how you say it. In *2015 11th IEEE International Conference and Workshops on Automatic Face and Gesture Recognition (FG)* (Vol. 1, pp. 1–6). https://www.cs.rochester.edu/~gildea/pubs/naim-fg15.pdf

Neave, Lucy; Connor, James, & Crawford, Amanda. (2007). *Arts of publication: Scholarly publishing in Australia and beyond*. Australian Scholarly Publishing.

Nicol, Donna J., & Yee, Jennifer A. (2017). "Reclaiming our time": Women of color, faculty and radical self-care in the academy. *Feminist Teacher, 27*(2–3), 133–156.

O'Cathain, Alicia; Murphy, Elizabeth, & Nicholl, Jon. (2008). Multidisciplinary, interdisciplinary, or dysfunctional? Team working in mixed-methods research. *Qualitative Health Research, 18*(11), 1574–1585.

Orazbayeva, Balzhan; Plewa, Carolin; Davey, Todd, & Muros, Victoria Galan. (2019). The future of university-business cooperation: Research and practice priorities. *Journal of Engineering and Technology Management, 54*, 67–80, https://hal.science/hal-02880384v1

Osipow, Samuel. (2006). Dealing with journal editors and reviews. In Fredrick T. L. Leong & James T. Austin (Eds.), *The psychology research handbook: A guide for graduate students and research assistant*, pp. 381–386. (2nd ed.) Sage.

Paltridge, Brian. (2017). *The discourse of peer review: Reviewing submissions to academic journals*. Springer. https://doi.org/10.1057/978-1-137-48736-0

Phillips, Matthew J.; Dzidic, Peta L.; Roberts, Lynne D., & Castell, Emily L. (2023). "Comply, strategise, or resist?": Exploring early-career women's academic identities in Australian higher education using Foucauldian discourse analysis. *SN Social Sciences, 3*(81), 1–38, https://doi.org/10.1007/s43545-023-00668-w

Pommerening, Arne. (2021). *Staying on top in academia: A primer for (self-)mentoring young researchers in natural and life sciences*. Springer Cham. https://doi.org/10.1007/978-3-030-65467-2

Price, Emma; Coffey, Brian, & Nethery, Amy. (2015). An early career academic network: What worked and what didn't. *Journal of Further and Higher Education, 39*(5), 680–698, https://doi.org/10.1080/0309877X.2014.971106

Randa, Moreoagae Bertha. (2023). Of wellbeing and self-care in academia. In Ida Fatimawati Adi Badiozaman, Voon Mung Ling & Kiran deep Sandhu (Eds.), *Women practicing resilience, self-care and wellbeing in academia*, pp. 186–198. Routledge. https://doi.org/10.4324/9781003341482-18

Richardson, Julia; Wardale, Dorothy, & Lord, Linley. (2019). The 'double-edged sword' of a sessional academic career. *Higher Education Research & Development, 38*(3), 623–637, https://doi.org/10.1080/07294360.2018.1545749

Roche, Joseph. (2022). *Essential skills or early career researchers*. Sage.

Roberts, Laura W., & Hilty, Donald M. (2017). *Handbook of career development in academic psychiatry and behavioral sciences*. (2nd ed.) American Psychiatric Association.

Russ-Eft, Darlene; Sleezer, Catherine M.; Sampson, Gregory, & Leviton, Laura. (2017). *Managing applied social research: Tools, strategies, and insights*. John Wiley & Sons.

Sauermann, Henry; Franzoni, Chiara, & Shafi, Kourosh. (2019). Crowdfunding scientific research: Descriptive insights and correlates of funding success. *PLoS One, 14*(1), e0208384, https://doi.org/10.1371/journal.pone.0208384

References

Schriever, Vicki, & Grainger, Peter. (2019). Mentoring an early career researcher: Insider perspectives from the mentee and mentor. *Reflective Practice, 20*(6), 720–731, https://doi.org/10.1080/14623943.2019.1674272

Siltanen, Janet; Willibi, Alette, & Scobie, Willow. (2008). Separately together: Working reflexively as a team. *International Journal of Social Research, 11*(1), 45–61, https://doi.org/10.1080/13645570701622116

Singh, Jasvir Kaur Nachetar (Ed.). (2022). *Academic mobility and international academics: Challenges and opportunities*. Emerald. https://doi.org/10.1108/9781801175104

Spina, Nerida; Harris, Jess; Bailey, Simon, & Goff, Mhorag. (2020). *'Making it' as a contract researcher: A pragmatic look at precarious work*. Routledge.

Starbuck, Wiliam H. (2003). Turning lemons into lemonade: Where is the value in peer reviews? *Journal of Management Inquiry, 12*(4), 344–351, https://doi.org/10.1177/1056492603258972

Starks, Donna, & Robertson, Margaret J. (2024). *Fifty things to think about when writing your thesis: Paving your way to submission*. Routledge.

Sum, Nicola. (2023). Solitude, sanctuary, and pseudo-mentors: A pandemic lens on an early career transition into doing and being research/researcher. In In Ida Fatimawati Adi Badiozaman, Voon Mung Ling & Kiran deep Sandhu (Eds.), *Women practicing resilience, self-care and wellbeing in academia*, pp. 57–68. Routledge. https://doi.org/10.4324/9781003341482-18

Svantesson, Eleonor; Senorski, Eric Hamrin; Samuelsson, Kristian, & Karlsson, Jón. (2019, online). Common mistakes in manuscript writing and how to avoid them. In Musahl Volker et al. (Eds.), *Basic methods handbook for clinical orthopaedic research*, pp. 579–584. Springer. https://doi.org/10.1007/978-3-662-58254-1

Ta, Binh; Hoang, Cuong; Khong, Hang, & Dang, Trang. (2024). Australian PhD graduates' agency in navigating their career pathways: Stories from social sciences. *Higher Education, 88*,1525–1545, https://doi.org/10.1007/s10734-024-01181-6

Thomas, David R., & Hodges, Ian H. (2010). *Designing and managing your research project: Core skills for social and health research*. Sage. https://doi.org/10.4135/9781446289044

Thwaites, Rachel, & Pressland, Amy. (Eds.). (2017). *Being an early career feminist: Academic global perspectives, experiences and challenges*. Palgrave Macmillan. https://doi.org/10.1057/978-1-137-54325-7

Tullu, Milind. S. (2019). Writing the title and abstract for a research paper: Being concise, precise, and meticulous is the key. *Saudi Journal of Anaesthesia, 13*(1), S12–S17, DOI: 10.4103/sja.SJA_685_18

Voight, Michael L., & Hoogenboom, Barbara J. (2012). Publishing your work in a journal: Understanding the peer review process. *International Journal of Sports Physical Therapy, 7*(5), 452–456.

Wald, Navé; Kumar, Vijay, & Sanderson, Lara J. (2023). Enhancing co-supervision practice by setting expectations in a structured discussion using a research-informed tool. *Higher Education Research & Development, 42*(3), 757–769, https://doi.org/10.1080/07294360.2022.2082390

Westra, Daan, & Fleuren, Bram. (2022). To come, to see, to conquer: Practical pointers in applying for funding and securing your initial grants. In Dominika Kwasnicka & Alden Yuanhong Lai (Eds.), *Survival guide for early career researchers*, pp. 119–129. Springer International.

Wheat, Rachel. E.; Wang, Yiwei; Byrnes, Jarrett. E., & Ranganathan, Jai. (2013). Raising money for scientific research through crowdfunding. *Trends in Ecology & Evolution, 28*(2), 71–72, https://dx. doi.org/10.1016/j.tree.2012.11.001

Williams, Alison; Jones, Derek, & Robertson, Judy (Eds.). (2014). *BITE: Recipes for remarkable research*. Brill.

Wisker, Gina, & Robinson, Gillian. (2013). Doctoral 'orphans': Nurturing and supporting the success of postgraduates who have lost their supervisors. *Higher Education Research & Development, 32*(2), 300–313, https://doi.org/10.1108/17597511311316982

Wrosch, Carsten; Miller, Gregory. E.; Scheier, Michael F., & De Pontet, Stephanie Brun. (2007). Giving up on unattainable goals: Benefits for health? *Personality and Social Psychology Bulletin, 33*(2), 251–265, https://doi.org/10.1177/0146167206294905

Yeo, Marie, & Lewis, Marilyn. (2019). Co-authoring in action: Practice, problems and possibilities. *Iranian Journal of Language Teaching Research, 7*(3), 109–123, https://doi.org/10.30466/ijltr.2019.120739

Zhu, Yimei, & Procter, Rob. (2015). Use of blogs, Twitter and Facebook by UK PhD students for scholarly communication. *Observatorio, 9*(2), 29–46.

Zimmerman, Aaron Samuel. (2021). *Methodological innovations in research and academic writing*. IGI Global. https://doi.org/10.4018/978-1-7998-8283-1

Index

Note: Page numbers followed by "n" refer to end notes.

abstract 52–54, 58–61, 81–82
Artificial Intelligence (AI) 149–151

book: chapters 12, 13, 23, 52–54, 98; contracts 51, 53; proposals 50, 130; publishers 50, 53, 58, 117; publishing 43, 49; time 51–53
brand: developing 16, 19–21, 24–25, 33, 45, 115; institutional 32, 42–43, 54
budget: apps 85; categories 85–86; contracts 87; expenses 77, 85; flexibility 86, 122; staff turnover 87; tasks 23, 82, 85–91; workshops 50; see also change; funding; grants

career: decision making 4, 10, 19, 35, 147; planning 10, 13, 18, 27, 40, 41, 45, 104, 135; progression 17, 37, 57, 139–141; success 19, 21, 27–29, 33–34, 41, 47; trajectory 42, 45, 54, 131, 136; transition 142–144; see also change
change: budget 91; career 10, 36, 43, 142–144; research 5, 11, 19, 42; see also identity
co-authoring: difficulties 107–119; forms 28, 33–34, 48; power dynamics13, 63; supervisee 102–104

co-supervision: expectations 101–102, 125; policy 100; team members 100–101, 124; topics 96; see also ways
committee: choosing 40; membership 41; visibility 40
community research: gatekeepers 71, 86; giving back 72–73; research interviews 42, 87, 91, 122
conferences: costs 26–27; format 25–26; size 25–26; timeslots 31n3; uses 24–27, 38, 53, 97; see also online
crowdfunding: donors 78, 79; platforms 78–79; public interest 79, 80, 82; timelines 80; reviews 78; see also research

difficulties: co-authoring 107–109; doctoral orphan 126–128; grants 119–123; manuscripts 110–112; publication 112–119; supervision 123–126

ECR: unique 17–19
employment: casual 132–134, 144; contract 17, 57, 68, 136; government 17, 28, 75, 143, 144; industry 17, 143, 144; NGO 17, 144; sessional 75, 132–134

Index

equipment 23, 77, 85–87, 122
extra-curricular activities 131

feedback: critical friend 60–62, 64, 111; inspiration 65; reviewer 51, 54, 59, 60, 62, 65, 103, 114–116; sequence 61; *see also* types
funding: applications 68–70, 76–78; large scale 76, 88–91; new projects 77; research without 69–71; sources 67; *see also* budget; types

grants: external 28, 40, 75, 84; internal 74–75, 123; management 88–91; success 17; *see also* budget
guidebooks 2–4

Hay, Iain 71, 132

identity: emerging 13; imagined 13, 19, 21, 45, 123; leading your team 73, 88, 89; supervision 1, 94, 95, 105n1, 123, 148; transformative 1, 3
impact: advertising 22, 89, 90; expertise 22, 40, 48, 54, 83, 97, 130; outside academia 4, 41, 48, 78, 102
inside knowledge 143
Instructions to Authors 117
introduction: paragraph 59, 82; section 59, 61, 110, 118

job interview 5, 137–139
journals: general submission 49, 53–55; mentors 46, 57; processes 49, 51, 54, 57; response time 57; reviewers 57–60, 62, 64–65, 113–116; special issues 49, 52–53; *see also* types

key terms 46, 59, 61
Khoo, Tseen 3, 75, 78

leading your team: gratitude 89–90; keeping on track 90; meetings 90; team dynamics 89; websites 90; *see also* identity
letter: cover 131, 132; editor 48, 114–116
literature review 56, 70, 91, 95, 99, 110, 117, 118
lived experiences 10–11, 72, 83, 94, 130–132, 143

manuscripts: publication types 49–55; time 51–54; word limits 56, 59, 117, 119; *see also* difficulties; types
marking 132, 133, 144
methodology 11, 61, 81, 99, 100, 110, 120
mentors: finding 35–37; location 36; trust 35; *see also* types

networks: personal 24, 79; professional 23, 36–39; support 37–39, 42; *see also* online

O'Donnell, Jonathan 3, 75, 78
online: conference 26; support groups 38, 39; safety 30, 31; supervision 97, 98; surveys 18, 70, 71, 122

paragraph 20, 48, 82, 110, 115, 117, 118, 130
perfectionism 111
policy 42, 48, 100
positions: ideal 27, 28; location 28, 133; research links 28, 74; moving 28; preferred institution 28
post-docs 86, 87, 134–136
principal supervisor 100, 101, 123–125
promotion 139–142
publishing: risk-taking 18; thesis 5, 10–11, 19, 45–46; timelines 46, 50, 51; *see also* types

quotes 63

Index

referees 56, 131, 137; reference check 137
research: agenda 18, 135; question 11, 20, 70, 71; profile 76, 80, 84; safety 29–31; teams 68–70, 72, 73, 82; unfunded 69–71
research candidates: best match 94, 96–98, 126; preparedness 94, 98; research capabilities 94; research profile 20, 96–97
resilience 136–139
review process 112–114; reviewers 51, 54, 55, 59, 60, 62, 65, 82
Robertson, Margaret J. 46, 50, 64, 103, 118

scaling down 70
selling: ideas 24–27, 80–83; yourself 21–23, 83
shortlist 137
social networks 20, 22–24; uses 22; *see also* types
Starks, Donna 46, 50, 64, 103, 118
Supervision 17, 93–105, 123–128; co-supervisors 100–102, 123–126; data ownership 103; initial meetings 98–99; supervising 93–105; successful 98–101; taking over 126–127; *see also* co-supervision; identity; online
support groups: academic 42, 48; multidisciplinary 3; professional 22, 30; purpose 22, 38, 39, 111; *see also* online
surveys 70

teaching 5, 17, 28, 81, 130, 132–133
thesis: reworking 10, 50; transitioning from 10–11
time 11, 17, 113, 117, 121, 127, 146–147; time management 112, 131; timelines 46, 69, 77, 80; time poor 5, 103, 111
title 55, 58, 60, 80–81
travel 85, 86, 122
types: brands 19–21, 42–43; collaborations 32–43; feedback 14, 40, 60–62, 94, 111; funding 76–80; manuscripts 49–56; mentors 35–37; social networks 21–24

voice 62–64

Ward, Phil 3, 75, 78
ways: being 12–13, 18, 23, 35, 95, 111; communicating 13–14, 23, 38, 62–63, 95, 133; doing 12–13, 18, 23, 35, 95, 111; knowing 11–12, 40, 63, 84, 91, 143; supervising 94–95
wellbeing 29–31, 145–148; family 27, 133, 142; mental health 18, 24, 33, 107, 124; physical health 29, 31, 146, 147; safety 29–31; trauma 30; *see also* online
workload 40, 101, 107, 125
writing: audience 23, 25, 58, 79; personalize 60, 64; *see also* selling

For Product Safety Concerns and Information please contact our EU
representative GPSR@taylorandfrancis.com
Taylor & Francis Verlag GmbH, Kaufingerstraße 24, 80331 München, Germany

www.ingramcontent.com/pod-product-compliance
Lightning Source LLC
Chambersburg PA
CBHW052342230426
43664CB00042B/2697